THE
EBOLA OUTBREAK
IN WEST AFRICA

Corporate Gangsters, Multinationals & Rogue Politicians

CHERNOH ALPHA M. BAH

Philadelphia

THE Ebola outbreak IN West Africa
Corporate Gangsters, Multinationals & Rogue Politicians

Africanist Press books may be ordered through booksellers or by contacting:
Africanist Press
5114 Race Street
Philadelphia, PA 19139
www.africanistpress.com

+1-301-476-1226 (United States)
+1-208-709-4140 (United States)
+ 232 – 76 -757924 (Sierra Leone)
Email: africanists@yahoo.com

ISBN 978-0-9969739-0-8 (e)
ISBN 978-0-9969739-2-2 (sc)
ISBN 978-0-9969739-1-5 (hc)

Printed in the United States of America.

Dedicated to the everlasting memory of:
Comrade Alhaji Seray Bah
(Journalist, broadcaster and human rights advocate)
You are gone but your spirit shall live on

CONTENTS

FOREWORD

The worst outbreak of the Ebola Virus Disease in history (affecting primarily Guinea, Liberia and Sierra Leone) seems now to be abating; and by the end of July 2015, the United Nations closed down its Ebola mission, UNMEER, to be followed in quick succession by several other international efforts. Because the countries primarily affected are weak and poor, with incompetent and corrupt governments, they have for the past decade been the magnet for all kinds of international activity, good and bad. Not surprisingly, the outbreak was devastating. Tens of thousands of people were affected, and thousands died.

At the height of the outbreak in August 2014, the *New York Times* carried a prominent story on the Sierra Leonean activist and opposition politician Chernoh Alpha M. Bah. He had brought in a container packed with donated items from the United States, including protective gowns, gloves, stretchers, mattresses and other medical supplies needed to help fight the epidemic in his country. Instead, the container was held up at the port for over two months, while in his hometown of Makeni (which also happens to be President Ernest Bai Koroma's hometown) – the *New York Times* helpfully reported – a surge of Ebola cases had "quickly overwhelmed health workers, with protective gear so lacking that some nurses have worked around the deadly virus in their street clothes." After this high-profile intervention, so to speak, the government cleared the container, and Mr. Bah made sure its contents were quickly made available to health workers and Ebola patients in the country.

The Ebola outbreak in West Africa: Corporate Gangsters, Multinationals & Rogue Politicians is Mr. Bah's immensely timely and well-documented effort to understand how and why the Ebola calamity happened, and why governments in the region, particularly that of his own country, were so tragically unprepared to meet the challenge. I cannot bet, however, that the *New York Times*, whose support was so critical to the author during his standoff with his country's chronically graft-addled and incompetent government, will be altogether pleased with the book. For here, Mr. Bah's sharp unforgiving words are directed not just against his government, but also against major Western institutions and some of the murderous policies and actions of Western governments and scientists towards Africans.

For Mr. Bah is much more than a politician – a category that in his country and region is dominated by some of the most fickle and unprincipled hustlers imaginable. He is one of a dying breed: a solid Pan Africanist and socialist, and an articulate social critic and humanist. I have followed his work with great admiration for over a decade, which is why I feel honored to contribute a Foreword to this book.

The book at first glance will strike some as hasty and polemical; but I implore the reader to persist through its passionate but thoughtful and reasoned pages to the end. The author marshals persuasive evidence to justify his claims, and he is careful about making unwarranted allegations. I feel enriched by its contents.

In an interview by the journal *Science* (published in October 2014), Dr. Oyewale Tomori, the president of the Nigerian Academy of Science, and that country's leading virologist, made the following comments about the Ebola crisis then at its height: "I wish I could say with confidence that in 10 years' time we will not be where we are now with Ebola. But the countries have totally lost control of what is going on. If you go to Sierra Leone or Liberia today, there must be at least 10 international groups there. At the end of this epidemic, everybody will pack their bags and leave. The African countries will be left not really knowing what has happened to them. Like someone hit them smack in the face, totally disoriented. There will be millions of scandals about how money was misspent and so on. We will focus on those and move on. Ten years from now, people will have forgotten that there was Ebola and we will be back to where we started."

Dr. Tomori bemoaned West Africa's wilful lack of preparedness for the disease, and suggested that part of it has to do with our failure to ask hard uncomfortable questions, and make difficult decisions.

With this valuable book, Mr. Bah has begun asking those questions. One hopes that his will not be a lonely voice. For the sake of the thousands of lives lost, and to prevent a repeat of the calamity, one hopes that these sober and deeply felt reflections by an important witness will become a clarion call for action. Those who were complicit in the tragedy (local politicians and foreign 'scientists') must be made to account for the heinous crimes committed against our people.

Dr. Lansana Gberie
New York

Dr. Gberie is the author of the book, *A Dirty War in West Africa: the RUF and the Destruction of Sierra Leone* (Indiana University Press 2005) and most recently, *War, Politics and Justice in West Africa* (SLWS 2015).

PREFACE

FROM MILIANDOU TO KOINDU: INVESTIGATING EBOLA'S ORIGIN AND TRANSMISSION CHAIN

Our first duty is to uncover, and confront, the full truth about what happened...[1]
- Kofi Annan, *former United Nations Secretary General*

I was out of the country when the "Ebola outbreak" began in West Africa. I had just published my book, *Neocolonialism in West Africa* in 2014[2] and had embarked on an international book tour across the United States and Europe a few months before the virus was reported in Sierra Leone. Reports of the horrible deaths and infections caused by the emerging outbreak quickly appeared on the frontline reports of western media organizations. They conveyed graphic and horrifying images of infected and dead persons. Along with these media reports, questions regarding the inadequate capacity of the health systems in the region to respond to the unfolding catastrophe also emerged.

In Sierra Leone, for example, local newspapers and radio stations reported a rising number of deaths among healthcare workers who appeared to be besieged by an unprecedented outbreak. They lacked all the required protective response equipment. Nearly all the public health facilities in Sierra Leone lacked basic protective equipment and essential facilities to respond to an outbreak: gloves, masks, stretchers, gowns, protective suits, and related equipment were absent.

---

[1] UN Secretary-General Kofi Annan's message to the ceremony marking the tenth anniversary of the Srebrenica massacre, delivered by Mark Malloch Brown, Chef de Cabinet, in Potocari-Srebrenica, July 11, 2005 (www.un.org/press/en/2005/sgsm9993.doc.htm).

[2] Chernoh Alpha M. Bah, *Neocolonialism in West Africa: A Collection of Essays & Articles* (Bloomington: iUniverse: Bloomington, 2014).

In the wake of the outbreak, doctors and nurses complained of a severe lack of medical equipment. Alarms were raised by sections of the independent media on the need for the required medical supplies and equipment to respond to the emerging outbreak. A nightline radio discussion in Freetown reported chilling accounts of how outbreak responders in some parts of Kailahun district, for example, used a single stretcher to transport both the dead and the newly infected.[3] In Kenema, nurses said the number of infected persons that trooped into the Kenema Government Hospital overwhelmed the capacity of the Ebola Treatment Center. Despite the continued complaints, the political elites felt comfortable and denied the severity of the outbreak. By this time, death numbers and infections were steadily rising in the Kailahun and Kenema districts, in the eastern part of the country.

I returned to Sierra Leone to assist in the national effort to fight the Ebola epidemic. Two weeks after my arrival, the country's leading virologist, Dr. Sheikh Umarr Khan, who was heading the fight against the outbreak, died; the outbreak claimed its first high profile victim in Sierra Leone. Suddenly, Sierra Leone and the Ebola epidemic dominated world headlines. Khan's death marked a change in the government's response to the outbreak. The morning of Khan's death, international airlines announced cancellations of flight operations into Sierra Leone. The government of Sierra Leone also announced a public health emergency in the country with a string of regulations: soldiers and police officers were now empowered to support health workers in the search for Ebola patients. Checkpoints and roadblocks were erected across the country, followed by several quarantined measures and restrictions on freedom of movement. It appeared Khan's death had changed the country; the Ebola outbreak was now very close to everybody. Reports of deaths and sporadic infections caused widespread panic across the country.

The deadly reality of the ongoing tragedy came very close to my eyes on October 21, 2014. That morning I received a phone call from a comrade in the diamond-mining district of Kono in eastern Sierra Leone, reporting the explosion of an Ebola related protest in the area. Medical staffs at the poorly equipped public hospital in the township were being chased by protesting youth and fleeing for their lives. Local residents reported witnessing deaths amid the riots. The specific numbers of casualties could not be determined that morning, but local authorities called in the police. A daytime curfew was imposed followed by several arrests. One of those arrested was a friend whose family had called me, crying for help. They reported that random and brutal police raids on communities accused of resisting Ebola health workers sparked the protests, which led to the arrests of scores of youths in the township.

---

[3] One such radio show was DJ Base's Nightline Program aired on AYV Radio FM 101.6 in Freetown.

Minutes after this disturbing phone call from Kono, news also came to me that a total of five health workers (two doctors and three nurses) had died overnight at a private clinic in Allentown (the community in Freetown), where I lived. The United Council of Imams, an Islamic group that provided community health care in Allentown, ran the clinic. Families of the deceased health workers reportedly went into hiding to avoid arrests and quarantine after reports emerged that the deaths of the health workers were related to Ebola. The deceased healthcare workers were said to have treated an Ebola patient a few days earlier. After a doctor died at the clinic's holding ward, several other patients who were receiving treatment at the clinic for other illnesses also went into hiding that same night. The entire Allentown community was engulfed with fear. A state of panic gripped residents. Nobody knew the total number of neighbors who had come in contact with the dead health workers, their surviving relatives, or the clinic's fleeing patients. The deadly Ebola virus had come too close to everyone in our neighborhood.

The following morning, October 22, 2014, more devastating news unfolded. A friend phoned me announcing the sudden death of two of her younger brothers in the neighboring Kosso Town community, also in east Freetown, a five-minute drive from Allentown. The woman reported that the two deaths, which occurred an hour apart from each other, were confirmed Ebola positive.

The news was very agonizing; a sense of despair, of pain, and of grief rang in her voice. It was more than a tragic loss. Over fifteen years ago, rebels killed her father and mother during the war. Two years before the Ebola outbreak, she also lost a son, who died of malaria before his third birthday. Later, when the obituary of her two brothers was announced in succession, she cried, "I am finished." Because she cared for her two brothers when they first complained of symptoms of malaria (which entail many of the same signs and symptoms as Ebola) she was alone in her grief as sympathetic neighbors stood at a distance, afraid to get too near to her for risk of the virus.

The Jui – Allentown axis, where she and her brothers lived, was now the hottest spot for Ebola deaths within the western area of the country. The deaths occurred just forty-eight hours after the initial deaths at the Islamic community clinic in Allentown. And about ten additional deaths would be reported within the Allentown community alone in the following twenty-four hours.

Residents of the Jui and Allentown communities also reported swelling numbers of new inhabitants who had come fleeing Ebola hotspots in Waterloo, a rural district of Freetown. They were escaping a planned lockdown of the Waterloo area by state authorities following scores of unprecedented deaths. The scenario was all too familiar to the residents who experienced similar chaos during the events of January 6, 1999, when rebels invaded Freetown.

Before my return to Sierra Leone in July 2014, however, I and a colleague based in Maryland in the United States who heads a charity organization named, Patriotic Care Sierra Leone[4] had launched an appeal for support to assist Ebola frontline workers in Sierra Leone with the needed basic protective equipment in the fight against the outbreak. Through our various contacts in the United States, we were able to mobilize a total of four forty-feet containers of medical supplies (face masks, hospital linens, stretchers, gloves, mattresses, and wheel chairs). The equipment totaled an approximated value of half a million United States dollars.

I sent an e-mail correspondence to government officials in Freetown through Oswald Hanciles, one of the presidential advisers of the government of Sierra Leone, at the State House. I notified them of the equipment we had mobilized and requested that, based on the emergency situation in the country, we wanted the government of Sierra Leone to assume responsibility for the shipping, clearing, and delivery of the equipment to the affected areas. I attached, with the originating correspondence, a list of all the equipment that had been loaded in the four forty-feet containers that awaited shipment to Freetown from Pennsylvania in the United States. On receipt of the said correspondence, Mr. Hanciles forwarded the matter for actions to all relevant authorities in government: senior officials at the State House, the Sierra Leone Ministry of Health, those at the Central Medical Stores, the Pharmacy Board of Sierra Leone, the Finance Ministry, and others at the president's office became involved in the discussions regarding the containers of medical equipment. Dozens of e-mails were exchanged between government officials in Freetown. The discussion centered on the payment of US$6,183 shipping fees by the government of Sierra Leone to have the first forty-feet container of medical equipment (valued over US$141,000) that arrived in the country on August 9, 2014, cleared and distributed.

Over fifty meetings and dozens of other e-mails between myself, Oswald Hanciles and many other officials (from State House to the Health Ministry) occurred for a period of two months, and the government of Sierra Leone refused to pay the shipping fees to get the container of much-needed supplies out of the Freetown seaport. This was now early October 2014. The death statistics on both health workers and ordinary people continually swelled, with hundreds being infected on a daily basis. On October 4th alone, the country reported a total of one hundred and forty deaths due to the outbreak. A *New York Times'* article published on October 1, 2014, contained detailed images of the gruesome deaths in a hospital in Makeni, the home of President Ernest Koroma.[5] The

---

[4] Patriotic Care-Sierra Leone is a private philanthropic charity registered and run by Mohamed L. Bah, a reputable Sierra Leonean businessman based in Maryland, USA. At the time of the Ebola outbreak, he served as the Fullah Progressive Union (FPU) president in Maryland and was also actively involved in several African initiatives geared towards community developments in Africa.

[5] Adam Nossiter, "A Hospital From Hell, in a City Swamped by Ebola," *New York Times*, October 1, 2014 (www.nytimes.com/2014/10/02/world/africa/ebola-spreading-in-west-africa.html).

article reported how healthcare workers in the township, overwhelmed by the volume of sick people and those who had died, were facing the disease in their street clothes with no protection. The graphic images in the *New York Times'* article were alarming. At this time, all our efforts to get the government to clear and deliver the consignment of medical supplies had failed. Then on October 5, 2014, the story of the container of medical supplies became the centerpiece of global media discussion: Adam Nossiter, the *New York Times'* West Africa correspondent, reported how government officials blocked the delivery of the said container through their refusal to pay the required shipping fees[6]. Nossiter's report revealed that the delay was caused by the government's effort to prevent an opposition political contender and critic of the president from scoring "political points" with the shipment. This was rightly the case. President Ernest Bai Koroma of Sierra Leone and myself had no love lost between us since he had assumed power. Between 2010 and 2012, I had constantly opposed his handling of state affairs and the pervasive corruption in his government. In 2012, I contested against his party in a constituency in Makeni for a parliamentary seat: the questionable results placed me second among seven other political contenders, including a candidate of Koroma's party. Since the end of the 2012 elections, I had openly stated that the election results that gave Koroma a second presidential term did not reflect the actual votes of the masses in the 2012 elections.

When my correspondence on the container of medical supplies reached State House, senior government officials in the president's office in Freetown reportedly debated the possible political implications of the donation. In private, personal communications, they argued on the potential "political capital" that news of the shipment of medical supplies would generate for me. Oswald Hanciles, one of the officials involved in the discussion, attempted unsuccessfully to impress upon his colleagues in the president's office the need to clear the container.[7] His efforts were rebuffed. Eventually, however, the container story became the subject of international media discussion: the *New York Times'* cover story was picked up by the *BBC, Aljazeera, Washington Post,* and others. The government propaganda machinery represented by *Awareness Times*, a local newspaper owned by a presidential propagandist, deliberately launched an unsuccessful campaign of calumny to cover-up the government's failure to clear the container. Together with health ministry officials, the *Awareness Times* falsely claimed that the container had expired drugs after it was cleared from the ports. This was a blatant lie. For eleven days the controversy over the container and its equipment dominated local news headlines in Freetown. The container story, especially the government's failure to timely get

---

[6] Adam Nossiter, "Ebola Help is Nearby, but Delayed on the Docks," *New York Times*, October 5, 2014 (www.nytimes.com/2014/10/06/world/africa/sierra-leone-ebola-medical-supplies-delayed-docks.html).

[7] Oswald Hanciles, "Ebola Saboteurs and Diabolical Propagandists," Oswald Hanciles Column: October 8, 2014.

it out of the ports, became a critical reference in the national outbreak response: an indicator of the government's lack of genuine commitment and non-prioritization of its response to the outbreak.

By mid-October 2014, however, the outbreak approached its peak (although we did not know this at the time). Daily Ebola deaths and infections soared into the hundreds and were occurring everywhere in the country. It became obvious that months after Ernest Koroma issued the state of emergency the country's chances of survival continued to get bleaker by the day. Government officials in Freetown continuously blamed the high death statistics and infection numbers on cultural habits and lack of proper hygiene. The whole world watched as Ebola consumed entire communities in Sierra Leone, just as they had been consumed by war just a handful of years before.

In the midst of the daily sad stories of the outbreak, competing narratives around the origin of the disaster also emerged. Western scientists reported that the outbreak originated in Miliandou, a village in the southern region of Guinea. They identified the index case of the outbreak to be a two-year old boy from that village who reportedly died in early December 2013 after eating an "insectivorous free-tailed bat." Western scientists and journalists called the outbreak the result of a "zoonotic transmission:" meaning people's appetite for hunting and eating wild animals and birds as the cause of the disease.

Government officials in the Mano River countries of West Africa imposed sanctions against what they called the consumption of bushmeat. But across communities, ordinary people questioned the truthfulness of the mainstream narrative. They wondered why they had lived with wild animals and birds for several centuries and had even hunted them occasionally for food, but they had not been exposed to any outbreak. They doubted the accuracy of the claim that the outbreak was the result of animal or bird consumption. Many also did not believe the claim that the virus was transmitted through bodily fluids – the touching of the sick and the washing of the dead.

Towards December 2014, when the West African outbreak dominated world news headlines, the virus had become a sexually transmitted disease. Many of the so-called Ebola male survivors, discharged from treatment centers, reportedly infected their wives or girlfriends through sexual intercourse. WHO experts reported that the virus had been found to survive in the scrotum of the male sexual organ for a period of between six and nine months after a surviving male patient had been discharged from a treatment center.[8] Government officials warned against sexual intercourse with Ebola survivors. Some newspapers reported cases of certain court magistrates convicting Ebola male survivors who allegedly infected their partners, through sexual intercourse, after they were

---

8 WHO Interim Advice on the "Sexual Transmission of the Ebola Virus Disease" issued May 8, 2015 (www.who.int/reproductivehealth/topics/rtis/ebola-virus-semen/en/).

discharged from Ebola treatment centers.[9]

These developments raised a number of problematic questions: was Ebola a sexually transmitted disease? What is its actual origin? How was it actually transmitted? The desire to seek answers to these and many other questions generated my interest to investigate the outbreak. I wanted to find out its actual place of origin and its transmission agency.

I was in Sierra Leone throughout the outbreak. Apart from the container of medical supplies, I organized a number of community assistance programs to help quarantined families and children who had lost parents due to the outbreak. Since July 2014, when I returned to the country, I kept a daily journal of updates, recording daily events and community stories related to the outbreak. I distributed these updates to tens of thousands of people around the world via social media. They mainly contained reports of daily new infections and new deaths and the reactions of family members and friends to these sad events. Information in these updates was sent to me directly by affected families and community organizers, and the updates were filled with heart-wrenching accounts of death and loss: I then realized that the outbreak had claimed more lives in the region than was actually reported by health authorities.

Towards the end of December 2014, I embarked on a journey across the Mano River countries to investigate what western reporters, scientists, and local politicians called "the transmission chain of the outbreak" via its "original infections route." I investigated from Miliandou in the southern region of Guinea to Koindu in the eastern part of Sierra Leone. I wanted to find out how the virus, which western scientists claimed had germinated in Miliandou (a tiny village) had actually started and evolved into an international disaster. In particular, I was eager to find out the conditions of Miliandou and, most importantly, how the family of the index case had fared since the outbreak.

I left Freetown on December 23, 2014, to travel across the most affected countries in search of the transmission agency of the outbreak. First, I travelled from Freetown to Guinea, passing through the provinces of Sierra Leone on my way to Conakry, and I came face-to-face with familiar scenes I had known and witnessed over ten years before: military checkpoints, police officers, armed soldiers, and long queues of teeming people being screened by youths who held temperature checking machines. Had the war years returned? The only difference was that the security officers were not looking for insurgents, they were looking for sick people; people who showed signs of a fever or anything remotely associated with the symptoms of Ebola were arrested. There were over ten military checkpoints from Waterloo, in rural Freetown, to the Guinean border. At all of these checkpoints, those who operated the temperature checks were youths who

[9] Liz Szabo, "Liberian Woman Appears to have Contracted Ebola Through Sex with Survivor," *USA Today*, May 1, 2015 (www.usatoday.com/story/news/2015/05/01/ebola-survivor-sex/26698329/).

volunteered to be part of the fight against the outbreak. The scenes reminded me of the thousands of youths who were an active force in the insurgency that wrecked Sierra Leone in the 1990s. Many were conscripted into fighting factions and thrown into combat with no conventional military training. The Ebola epidemic reinvented the same scenario – many of the young people involved in the screening of travelers at checkpoints never received any basic healthcare training. They operated like healthcare vigilantes involved in the fight against an outbreak they had no knowledge of. In many ways they looked like the war vigilantes, like the child soldiers and armed teenagers during the rebel years who were forced into service and given Kalashnikovs rifles to fight in a war whose objectives they did not know nor understand.

Along the highway from Freetown to Conakry, countless numbers of ambulances swerved in both directions; they drove past us with supersonic speed with fumigated windows and blazing sirens that sounded like death bells. Makeshift structures, all newly built with tarpaulin and roundly fenced, were erected along all major points on the highway. They were boldly marked "Ebola Holding Centers" with huge signposts. Spread almost everywhere on the highway, they depicted the presence and wreckage of the epidemic on the rural scenery. The atmosphere of the countryside smelled of chlorine, a testament to the overwhelming nature of the epidemic and its vicious onslaught.

I travelled with two other companions as my research assistants: one journalist and one photographer from Freetown. When we arrived at a checkpoint near Portloko in the northwest of Sierra Leone, a soldier said he needed verification that we actually came from Freetown. He told us that people in the surrounding communities were banned from traveling outside of their localities. The surrounding communities of Portloko were declared "red zones" and considered "Ebola hotspots." Anyone coming from those areas was regarded a potential Ebola patient.

The president had imposed travel restrictions across districts two days before we left Freetown. In Freetown itself a house-to-house search for potential Ebola patients, part of the government's New Year and Christmas lockdown of the country, had commenced the day I left. The soldier said he was enforcing the president's order, but our driver insisted that he was finding an opportunity to ask for a bribe. How could we know the difference?

Stories of bribery and other corruption related activities are common with cross border travels in West Africa; the Guinea-Sierra Leone border was not an exception. Nearly everyone who travelled on that road testifies to paying a bribe to security officers on both sides of the border. Cross border extortion remains a major problem to regional integration in Africa.

Upon reaching Guinea, we witnessed every traveler crossing into the country being charged ten thousand Guinean francs. But, surprisingly, no temperature checks were administered, and we went straight into Conakry without coming across a single ambulance. Guinean officers in charge of checkpoints on the road to Conakry were more interested in their bribe collection than in controlling the outbreak. They had no concerns about potential Ebola patients. They were apparently not worried that travelers, including Sierra Leoneans like ourselves who had come from communities considered "Ebola hot spots," might be carrying the virus.

In Conakry, everyone went about business as usual. Taxis plied the city of Conakry with seven passengers – four in the back seat and three in the front along with the driver. This was the direct opposite of Freetown. Crowd-control measures that reduced the number of persons in taxis and other commercial vehicles were enforced by police and armed officers in all parts of Sierra Leone. In Guinea, nothing had changed with the outbreak; mosques performed burial rituals and relatives buried their dead in Conakry without the involvement of health workers. On Christmas Eve (December 24, 2014), I went around Conakry and visited several offices and public spaces. I found only two temperature machines in only two public places. At one location, the guard who operated the temperature machine seemed tired with the routine screening exercise and allowed people a free passage into the building. All international flights: Air France, Brussels Airlines, and Air Maroc, continued flight operations into Guinea's international airport unhindered. Public offices, hairdressing saloons, barbershops, boutiques, market centers, hotels, restaurants, shops, banks, and Internet cafes; all operated normal work schedules. One day I witnessed three separate funeral processions all without the involvement of health workers. I noticed that the government's response to the Ebola crisis in Guinea had not affected everyday life in the country. There was obviously no panic over the dead, no restrictions on public gatherings; people's movement across the country was not limited. There was no control over market hours. Yet the statistics on Ebola deaths and infections in Guinea was far below the other two countries in the Mano River region: Sierra Leone and Liberia.

I then wondered why the stringent military measures and population containment policies of the government of Sierra Leone, for example, had not succeeded in halting the spread and casualties of the outbreak. I was also puzzled why Guinea, a country that western scientists and journalists claimed recorded the first case of Ebola in West Africa and apparently lacked all of the precautionary measures applied in Sierra Leone, had minimal deaths and infections. Had the government of Sierra Leone deliberately exaggerated the size and disaster of the outbreak? Or had western scientists and western journalists missed the actual origin of the outbreak and its modes of transmission?

My journey to trace the origin of Ebola's transmission chain in West Africa led me from Conakry to Miliandou in the southern region of Guinea, and then into the Kailahun and Kenema districts in the eastern parts of Sierra Leone. I travelled through the same route that the so-called index case of the virus in

Sierra Leone (a traditional healer who was identified by western reporters as the first Ebola patient) had travelled after reportedly visiting Ebola infected relatives in Guinea where she was allegedly infected before returning to eastern Sierra Leone.[10] I interviewed hundreds of outbreak victims: those who lost relatives and others who were reportedly infected, taken to treatment centers, and eventually survived. I spoke to many professionals involved in the outbreak response in the Mano River countries: journalists, politicians, doctors, nurses, aid workers, ambulance drivers, burial workers, and community leaders. In total, I spoke to three thousand individuals in West Africa between December 2014 and March 2015. Each of these individuals offered a distinct, though oftentimes similar, experience dealing with the outbreak, whether as victims, responders, or frontline workers.

The stories of victims (those who lost family members to the outbreak) and so-called survivors of the virus were so heart-wrenching that they left an indelible scar on my memory. I still recall the story of a two-month-old baby named Aminata Lamin at the Hastings Ebola Treatment Center in Freetown on January 9, 2015. On that day, the center's coordinator, Dr. Santigie Sesay, presided over the discharge of twelve Ebola survivors. He announced to a group of journalists that among the group was a two-month old baby who had initially been brought to the treatment facility along with her mother. The doctor explained to the journalists that the child had to be discharged without her mother who was still reportedly responding to treatment at the center.

"Due to the current state of the mother, the baby will be handed over to the Ministry of Social Welfare, Gender and Children's Affairs," Dr. Sesay announced to the journalists. A few days later, however, investigations revealed that the child's mother had actually died a week before the baby was discharged.

Aminata's story was not unique. On December 31, 2014, British aid workers at the Kerry Town Ebola Treatment Center in the outskirts of Freetown also announced they could not find a home for a five-month old baby named Fatmata Fornah. Fatmata's parents had both died of Ebola, and her aunt, in whose care the mother had left her before she died four days earlier, was kicked out of her home by a landlord who feared that the child was Ebola positive and would potentially spread the virus in the household.

Fatmata's story depicted the predicament of thousands of other children whose parents died during the outbreak. On December 25, 2014, the WHO announced that about thirty thousand children were orphaned by Ebola in Sierra Leone alone and that five million children in the Mano River countries were out of school due to the outbreak.

"Some of these kids may never go back to school due to lack of support.

---

[10] "Ebola Outbreak in Sierra Leone Traced to Traditional Healer's Funeral," *London Daily Mail*, August 31, 2014. (www.dailymail.co.uk/news/article-2738904/Ebola-outbreak-Sierra-Leone-traced-single-traditional-healer-s-funeral-14-women-infected.html).

The Ebola epidemic has increased the number of teenage pregnancies in Sierra Leone; the victims are all girls of school going age," WHO officials reported.[11] This outbreak, then, was more than a disaster.

This book is, therefore, a partial record of my observations and interpretations of the many episodes and events that took place in Sierra Leone, Liberia, and Guinea during the entire period of the outbreak in West Africa. The content of this book is the direct result of a theoretical and empirical investigation of the deadly episodes, together with the individual and institutional forces that characterized and helped define one of the most recent human tragedies in modern history. The facts and the evidence enumerated in this book came principally from records of western media and academic sources, official papers of national and international policy makers, private correspondences of government officials and international aid workers, and historical documents obtained from several libraries and other archival sources in different parts of the world. I deliberately omitted or refused to include in this current text the direct personal testimonies of victims' families, Ebola survivors, and the eyewitness accounts of the many frontline responders (ambulance drivers, burial workers, and local nurses) whom I interviewed across West Africa. It is my hope, therefore, that this book will help to correct the atrocious information (from western scientists and journalists) which dominated global understanding of the 2014 West African outbreak within global academia. It is also my hope that this book will equally serve as a starting point in our efforts to understand the real origin and causes of the tragedy that claimed the lives of thousands of our friends, neighbors, and family members. Justice starts with uncovering the truth.

Chernoh Alpha M. Bah
Freetown

---

[11] WHO Report on "Ebola Orphans in West Africa" released on Christmas day, December 25, 2015.

West Africa

Mauritania
Nouakchott

Mali
Timbuktu

Niger
Lake Chad

Dakar
Senegal
Niamey

Banjul
Gambia
Bamako
Burkina Faso

Bissau
Ouagadougou
Nigeria

Guinea-Bissau
Guinea
Ghana
Benin

Conakry
Togo
Abuja

Freetown
Côte D'Ivoire
Lake Volta
Lagos

Sierra Leone
Abidjan
Accra

Monrovia
Lome

Liberia
Porto Novo

Atlantic
Ocean

Timeline of Major Events

1972

- The US' Center for Disease Control (CDC) establishes three research stations in eastern Sierra Leone to carry out field studies on the Lassa fever virus, a viral hemorrhagic fever similar to Ebola.

1979

- Dr. Aniru Conteh of Sierra Leone is recruited as the CDC team leader to study the Lassa fever virus in Sierra Leone.

DECEMBER 1989

- Civil war breaks out in Liberia after Charles Taylor's National Patriotic Front of Liberia engages the government of Dictator Samuel Doe.

1990s

- Sierra Leone enacts World Bank and International Monetary Fund Structural Adjustment Programs to liberalize trade, decrease public spending, and lift price controls in return for loans and to attract corporate investment.

MARCH 1991

- Civil war breaks out in Sierra Leone after Taylor-backed Revolutionary United Front attacks villages in the eastern Sierra Leone district of Kailahun.

2001

- Following the September 11 terrorist attacks in New York and the Anthrax incidents, the CDC and National Institutes of Allergy and Infectious Diseases (NIAID) reclassifies Lassa fever as the highest risk level for potential bioterrorism use.
- Subsequently, millions of defense dollars flow into Liberia, Guinea, and Sierra Leone, home to Lassa fever, for research and defense purposes.

JANUARY 2002

- Sierra Leone Civil War declared over.

AUGUST 2003

- Second phase of the Liberian Civil War effectively ends with Charles Taylor's resignation from presidency.

MARCH 2004

- US$2 million UN Special Court House is opened in Freetown for purposes of trying war criminals.

APRIL 2004

- Dr. Aniru Conteh, one of the world's leading viral hemorrhagic fever specialists, dies at the Kenema Government Hospital in eastern Sierra Leone of Lassa fever after an accidental needle stick.

SEPTEMBER 2007

- Ernest Bai Koroma (All People's Congress candidate) declares contested presidential victory over Solomon Berewa (incumbent Sierra Leone People's Party candidate).

FEBRUARY 2010

- US funded Viral Hemorrhagic Fever Consortium (VHFC) is established with a US $15 million contract to coordinate biodefence research projects in eastern Sierra Leone.

APRIL 2012

- Charles Taylor convicted of war crimes by UN Special Court.

NOVEMBER 2012

- Koroma wins second term.

DECEMBER 6, 2013

- Toddler Emile Ouamouno is supposedly infected with the Ebola virus while playing with and/or grilling and eating an insectivorous bat near his home in Meliandou, a village in southern Guinea.
- Emile, his sister, and his mother die shortly thereafter. The mother, eight months pregnant, dies seemingly from the complications of a miscarriage, a fact not mentioned by scientists and journalists investigating the outbreak.
- Despite coming in contact with his wife's blood and his sick children, Emile's father Etienne Ouamouno never becomes ill or exhibits symptoms of the virus, another fact that goes unreported.

2014

- Sierra Leone ranked 183rd out of 187 countries in the Human Development Index.
- Guinea ranked 179th.
- Liberia ranked 175th.

FEBRUARY 2014

- According to the World Health Organization (WHO), Sia Wanda Koniono of Kailahun crosses into Guinea for medical treatment for what was likely Ebola. A number of individuals she came in contact with later die of the virus, contradicting the official story of the virus originating in Guinea and spreading to Sierra Leone in May.

MARCH 22, 2014

- Guinean officials first officially identify Ebola as responsible for 60 recent deaths.

MARCH 30, 2014

- Liberia reports first two official cases of Ebola.

MAY 2014

- Official Sierra Leone records state this as the month when the first cases of Ebola arrived in the country after a traditional healer from Sierra Leone named Mendinor traveled to and from Guinea, bringing the virus home with her.
- Mendinor's daughter-in-law, Mammie Lebbie, falls ill after participating in Mendinor's funeral.
- After Lebbie's urine samples reportedly test positive for Ebola, she and ten other patients flee from the Koindu Community Health Center to avoid being quarantined.
- Mammie Lebbie is considered the first laboratory confirmed case of the virus in Sierra Leone.
- Lebbie remains in hiding with her husband and six children until January 2015, when it is revealed that she has completely recovered from her illness without medical treatment and that none of her family contracted her illness, despite living with and caring for her.

JUNE 2014

- Confirmed total cases reach nearly 800, confirmed total deaths reach nearly 500.

JULY 29, 2014

- Dr. Sheikh Umar Khan, Sierra Leone's leading viral hemorrhagic fever specialist, dies of Ebola in Kailahun, Sierra Leone, after international experts decide not to treat him with the experimental drug *ZMapp*, three bottles of which were located in Kailahun.
- The vials of *ZMapp* are picked up by the US Marine Corps in a chartered Russian helicopter and administered to Nancy Writebol and Kent Brantly, two American Ebola aid workers in Monrovia, Liberia. The aid workers survive.

JULY 30, 2014

- The Sierra Leone Government declares a state of emergency.
- Sierra Leone government deploys troops to enforce quarantine measures.

AUGUST 2014

- WHO declares the Ebola outbreak an "international public health emergency."
- Official death toll from the virus reaches 1,000.
- WHO announces official number of cases and deaths is "vastly" underestimated.
- WHO approves use of unproven drugs and vaccines.
- The Liberian Government declares a state of emergency.
- The Guinean Government declares a state of emergency.

SEPTEMBER 2014

- First of many curfews enacted in Sierra Leone to hinder outbreak.
- Confirmed cases reach 7,500, confirmed deaths reach 3,500.
- US announces the deployment of 3,000 military personnel to Liberia.
- Britain announces the deployment of 750 military personnel to Sierra Leone.

OCTOBER 2014

- Confirmed cases reach 14,000, confirmed deaths reach 5,000.
- China announces the deployment of 480 "elite" military personnel to the region.

NOVEMBER 2014

- Two-thirds of new cases are reported in Sierra Leone.

DECEMBER 2014

- Confirmed cases top 19,000, confirmed deaths top 7,500.
- Sierra Leone bans Christmas and New Year's celebrations.

JANUARY 2015

- Fabian Leendertz of the Robert Koch institute publishes his study "Investigating the Zoonotic Origin of the West Africa Ebola Epidemic" in the journal *Molecular Medicine*. The study claims that the virus started on December 6, 2013, in Miliandou, Guinea, when toddler Emile Ouamouno was infected while playing with and/or grilling and eating an insectivorous bat.
- Every major western news source endorses the Leendertz study.
- Confirmed cases reach 22,000, confirmed deaths top 8,800.

FEBRUARY 2015

- Confirmed cases top 24,000, confirmed deaths top 10,000.

APRIL 2015

- A deceased nine-month old is posthumously diagnosed as Ebola positive in Sierra Leone's Kailahun district, over 100 days since the district reported an Ebola case. Local politician Alex Bonapha challenges the diagnosis. The Sierra Leone government ridicules Bonapha before an investigation reveals the case to have been a misdiagnosis.

MAY 2015

- Official death toll recorded as 11,000.
- Liberia is officially declared Ebola free.
- An average of ten weekly cases continue in Sierra Leone.
- Dozens of weekly cases continue in Guinea.

AUGUST 2015

- WHO and UN official outbreak totals by country include:
    - Sierra Leone: 13,541 infections, 3,952 deaths.
    - Liberia: 10,672 infections, 4,808 deaths.
    - Guinea: 3,792 infections, 2,527 deaths.

INTRODUCTION

FROM CIVIL WAR TO EBOLA: A STORY OF HUMAN TRAGEDY

"The causes of most crises are political; some consequences may be humanitarian. But labeling them "complex emergencies" and "humanitarian crises" disconnects the consequences from the causes and permits the international response to be assigned – and confined – to the humanitarian domain. There are more lucid explanations for the increased humanitarian aid in today's conflicts than increased barbarity…"
— Fiona Terry, *Condemned to Repeat: The Paradox of Humanitarian Action*[12]

By the time the director general of the World Health Organization (WHO) declared the Ebola outbreak in West Africa a public health emergency of international concern (August 8, 2014), the virus was already at its murderous peak. An official death toll of nine hundred and thirty-two persons and over a thousand infections existed in the region around the time of this declaration. The epidemic had become a progressive human catastrophe in West Africa months ahead of the WHO's conclusion that the Ebola outbreak in the region constituted an "extraordinary event" with huge public health risks to other States.

Six months earlier, western scientists reported the appearance of the Ebola virus in an infant in Miliandou, a remote village in the Guekedou area, in southern Guinea. The scientists claimed that the epidemic originated from a single "zoonotic transmission" that involved this two-year old boy, whom they named as the conduit from which the virus passed from bats to humans before spreading via human-to-human contact. This resulted in a chain of transmissions that

---

[12] Fiona Terry, *Condemned to Repeat: The Paradox of Humanitarian Action* (London and Ithaca: Cornell University Press, 2002) p.13.

spread from the southern forests of Guinea into Sierra Leone and Liberia, leaving behind trails of dead and highly infectious, sick people.

With WHO's announcement, international news was now focused on West Africa's most volatile enclave – the Mano River countries of Guinea, Liberia, and Sierra Leone. Twenty years before this Ebola outbreak, these three countries attracted global media attention when images of the unprecedented atrocities of the civil wars and the huge numbers of refugees they created in the 1990s gripped the attention of world policy makers. The glamorized images of civilian amputees and gun-toting child combatants formed the centerpiece of western media coverage of the wars and the fleeing refugees. Hundreds of non-governmental organizations and aid agencies scrambled for space and resources in response to the unfolding humanitarian tragedy that emerged out of the violence of the wars in West Africa.

The West African wars of the 1990s inaugurated the largest United Nations military mission in world history[13]: Sierra Leone and Liberia became leading areas of interest for western political leaders, journalists, and aid organizations. But western media interests in the region quickly dissipated with the end of the brutal 1990s civil wars and the return to stability. More than twenty years later, troops of western journalists and scientists had found renewed interests in the region. The usual images of sick and dying Africans had once again appeared on western television. The usual western experts on African affairs, mostly far removed from the actual areas of the unfolding disasters, found new relevance, garnering huge amounts of face-time on television news to offer explanations on the origin of the virus and the causes of its unabated spread across international borders.

These western academics, politicians, journalists, doctors, and scientists offered multiple opinions on the exploding Ebola epidemic in West Africa: its origin, its strain, its mode of transmission, its potential for mutation, and the amount of resources required to contain it from spreading to "safe areas" of the world.

Western hysteria reached its highest point when incidental cases of infected persons started arriving in the United States from the affected countries. The WHO eventually announced, alongside its declaration on the Ebola epidemic, several international travel measures which called on states to "conduct exit screening of all persons at international airports, seaports and major land crossings, for unexplained febrile illness consistent with potential Ebola infection." This exit

---

[13] The United Nations Mission in Sierra Leone (UNAMSIL), whose initial mandate was to monitor and assist with the implementation of the Lomé Peace Agreement between the Sierra Leone government and RUF rebels was later changed by a UN Security Council Resolution, which empowered the military mission with the task to establish law and order throughout Sierra Leone. To help UNAMSIL carry out this new mandate, in February 2000, the Security Council increased the size of the UN military force to 11,100 troops, and by March 2001 it was further increased to 17,500 military personnel, which made it the UN's largest military operation at the time. See Adebajo, A. and D. Keen (2007), "Sierra Leone" in M. Berdal and S. Economides (eds.), *United Nations Interventionism, 1991-2004* (Cambridge: Cambridge University Press), pp.246-73.

screening, the WHO said, should consist of a questionnaire, a temperature mea-
surement and, if there is a fever, an assessment of the risk that the fever is caused
by the Ebola virus.

"Any person with an illness consistent with the Ebola virus should not be
allowed to travel unless the travel is part of an appropriate medical evacuation,"
officials of the World Health Organization said in a communiqué issued on
August 8, 2014.[14]

The virus quickly overwhelmed many communities with its attendant atrocious
consequences, destabilizing the entire region and forcing experts to consider the
2014 Ebola outbreak an "unprecedented disaster" in the region. At the time of the
WHO's declaration, hundreds of families and several communities were already
victims and witnesses to the virus and its horrific ravages. The stories of gruesome
deaths and the exploding chains of deadly infections they created quickly became
part of the terrific stories of daily life in Sierra Leone, Liberia, and Guinea.

Regional political authorities and their national health officials reportedly held
several meetings with some international health experts to determine the response
mechanisms to the unfolding disaster. Initially in Sierra Leone, however, when
reports of unprecedented deaths first emerged in the eastern district of Kailahun,
national officials denied the presence of the virus in the country.

The Sierra Leone government did not treat the unfolding epidemic with its
required seriousness.[15] The government's response to the outbreak was synony-
mous with its response to the start of the civil war; when reports that an armed
group had attacked villages in the eastern district of Kailahun in March of 1991,
they were dismissed as insignificant by ruling party officials in Freetown. Both
catastrophic events thus began for Sierra Leone in the district of Kailahun, and
both occurred under the administration of the All Peoples Congress (APC), the
political party that had ruled as a one party state for decades and was still in power
when the rebel war broke out in 1991. After initial reports of the virus in the
country, a government minister is believed to have told journalists that the death
reports were part of opposition propaganda designed to undermine support for
the government[16]. Serious government action was only taken several weeks into

---

[14] "Statement on the First Meeting of the IHR Emergency Committee on the 2014 Ebola outbreak in West Africa," *World Health Organization,* August 8, 2014 (www.who.int/mediacentre/news/statements/2014/ebola-20140808/en).

[15] Sheku Sheriff, "Ebola in Sierra Leone: Background on the Sacking of Miatta Kargbo" *H5N1,* August 31, 2014 (crofsblogs.typepad.com/h5n1/2014/08/ebola-in-sierra-leone-background-on-the-sacking-of-miatta-kargbo.html).

[16] See *Associated Press'* article from June 21, 2014: "Ebola outbreak: Sierra Leone Defends Response" quoting Sierra Leone's Deputy Information Minister, Theo Nicol, when he raises criticism over labeling the gov-ernment's response as "unfair and bias." (www.cbc.ca/news/world/ebola-outbreak-sierra-leone-defends-re-sponse-1.2683381). Laurie Garrett also cites reference to this comment in the article, "Sierra Leone's Ebola Epidemic Is Spiraling Out of Control" published by *Foreign Policy* on December 10, 2014 (foreignpolicy.com/2014/12/10/sierra-leones-ebola-epidemic-is-spiraling-out-of-control).

the outbreak and only after the high profile medical doctor Sheikh Umarr Khan reportedly died of Ebola in July of 2014.

Dr. Khan was a specialist in viral hemorrhagic diseases and one of the world's leading specialists on Lassa fever. He was head of the decades old twelve-unit Lassa Fever Ward and Research Program at the Kenema Government Hospital in eastern Sierra Leone. Weeks before his death, Khan appeared on national television and international media reporting his effort to combat the exploding Ebola outbreak in eastern Sierra Leone. His death from Ebola created panic across the country. The day after his death, government officials announced a national health emergency with a string of measures restraining free movement and public gatherings.

After Khan died, Ernest Bai Koroma, the president of Sierra Leone, announced a public health emergency in the country which included new executive orders empowering the police and army to support health workers in identifying and containing the chain of transmission. With Kahn's death and the horrific accounts of rising deaths and infections beginning to grip the attention of the local press in Freetown, some sections of the population were already blaming Koroma for his failure to seriously deal with the virus when it first began.

The president took five weeks to issue an official statement on the epidemic. He did not visit any of the areas affected by the disease until ten weeks into the outbreak and only did so after persistent pressure from the local press and other civil society activists. By that time, the Ebola Management Center in Kenema alone lost twenty-eight health workers, including two doctors and numerous nurses, lab technicians, and some ambulance drivers. In some of the referral hospitals across the country, health workers had gone on strike over non-payment of allowances and a lack of basic personal protective equipment. Many hospitals had no gloves, stretchers, and other isolation supplies needed by nurses and doctors caring for Ebola patients.

When he spoke about the situation on August 15, 2014, Koroma blamed the international community for the country's failure to confront the Ebola virus. "I am disappointed at the international community in their delay in responding towards the fight against the deadly Ebola virus in Sierra Leone. We have not been provided with enough equipment, resources, qualified health officers, and we have lost the only expert we had in the country to the disease amidst the declaration of the international health emergency on Ebola," Koroma said in a press release issued by the State House Communications Unit.[17]

The government was shifting away its responsibility to handle its own affairs. Casting blame on the international community for the deteriorating situation was indicative of Koroma's inability and unwillingness to deal with the emergency.

---

[17] Umaru Fofana, "Blaming WHO, Blaming Sierra Leone President," *Politico Newspaper*, August 21, 2014 (politicosl.com/2014/08/blaming-who-blaming-sierra-leone-president).

News of Ebola's presence in the region was reported months earlier, but the Sierra Leone government failed to adequately prepare for the unfolding catastrophe. The Association of Nurses and Sierra Leone Medical and Dental Association were never engaged by authorities to discuss the situation during the initial stages of the outbreak.

The government's priority was focused on other areas. Koroma and his party activists were planning a possible amendment to the national constitution to allot him a third-term in office. On April 27, 2014, during a road opening ceremony in Freetown, the president assured those advocating for a third term agenda on his behalf that they were exercising their rights to free speech. Tens of thousands of t-shirts were distributed to ruling party youths, and monies, amounting to millions of taxpayers' funds, had been spent on mobilization for the ceremony[18]. Barely a month later, Ebola spread across the country, unleashing a national nightmare. The government's inability or failure to rapidly and quickly respond to the unfolding catastrophe at its earlier stages would ultimately result in irreparable damage; countless deaths and infections quickly spread to every community in the country.

At the beginning of the outbreak, Sierra Leone's health ministry was totally unprepared. Civil Society groups complained of a lack of a comprehensive national strategy in response to the epidemic. During the early days of the outbreak Health workers in Sierra Leone reported that the stockpiled Ebola test kits were already expired. Along with test kits, the personal protective equipment (PPE) packets used by the health workers were totally inadequate for the Ebola response efforts. Even before Dr. Khan's death, several frontline health workers became infected and many died due to lack of protective gear and equipment. Basics such as facemasks, stretchers, mattresses, protective gloves, and other isolation supplies were missing.

When national measures were finally invoked to stem the crisis, they produced a mirage of efforts. Some diplomatic officials described the national response as chaotic: from songs to posters, billboards, and radio jingles, everybody wanted their contribution to be noticed. Politicians, musicians, clergymen, and religious heads were out contending for space in the humanitarian field opened up by the epidemic. These were in addition to a stream of international agencies consistently arriving in the country. The government established an Emergency Operations Center (EOC) to coordinate the patchwork of national agencies and international aid groups helping to battle the virus.

At the heart of the confusion, caused by this heterogeneous response, was the government's own effort to remain in command. A foreign diplomat described the national response in a *New York Times* report in early October of 2014 as

---

[18] Dominique JJ Tucker, "President Koroma Warns to Protect US$30M Road," *Africa Young Voices*, April 30, 2014 (africayoungvoices.com/2014/04/president-koroma-warns-to-protect-30m-grafton-road-no-heavy-truck-no-pan-body).

"a total mess." "Nobody appeared to be in charge at the agency, known as the Emergency Operations Center. Different factions made decisions independently," the official told the *New York Times*.[19]

A few months into the crisis, amidst growing criticism of the government's response, Sierra Leone's public officials took to blaming the ordinary people for the ongoing spread of the virus. They said the public would not give up their old cultural habits of touching the sick and washing the dead. But a senior Chinese official who visited the country told journalists that people lacked trust in the government's response mechanism. This, the Chinese official said, was responsible for people's failure to heed national messages of prevention put out by health officials. Both of these explanations missed the true reason for the devastation; the health infrastructure of Sierra Leone, like the other two affected countries, was in serious ruins for decades before the Ebola outbreak. The capacity of national authorities in West Africa to handle complex emergencies was non-existent. In the case of Sierra Leone, the political will and genuine commitment required from a government to deal with the unfolding tragedy were completely absent from the agenda of the administration.

Lack of trust in government was indeed not caused by the Ebola epidemic. It was a symptom of the crisis of leadership in the country. Corruption and graft are decades old characteristics of governance in Sierra Leone and the other Ebola affected countries in West Africa. Rich in mineral wealth and energy resources, the three affected countries are host to some of the largest multinational corporations engaged in the extraction of diamonds, gold, iron ore, aluminum, rubber, and petroleum resources[20]. These include Goodyear and Firestone (huge rubber operations in Liberia), Rio Tinto (mining in Guinea), and the Titanium Resources Group (also operating in Sierra Leone). Other corporate giants in the region are Alcoa, Alcan, Bollore Africa Logistics, African Minerals, London Mining, African Petroleum, DeBeers Corporation, Socfin International, and Vedanta; all engage in large-scale multinational resource exploitation in the sub-region. Corporate arrangements in all these countries represent a classic case of colonial exploitation.

Vast mineral wealth and energy resources are consistently looted at the expense of basic social and economic development in all three countries. The political elites, the equivalent of a state mafia, have sold out all of the strategic resources to multinationals and corporate henchmen for a loaf of bread without any regard for the devastating economic consequences of their neoliberal policies. The International Monetary Fund (IMF) and World Bank Structural Adjustment

---

[19] Adam Nossiter, "Ebola Help for Sierra Leone Is Nearby, but Delayed on the Docks," *New York Times*, October 5, 2014, (www.nytimes.com/2014/10/06/world/africa/sierra-leone-ebola-medical-supplies-delayed-docks.html).

[20] See Economic Development Reports of the United Nations Development Program (UNDP) and CIA Fact Book on Sierra Leone, Liberia, and Guinea.

Programs (SAPs) of the 1970s and 1980s promoted national initiatives that undermined social service delivery and economic growth. The privatization of essential social services like health care and education had a significant impact on human development in the region. Sierra Leone, Liberia, and Guinea occupy the leading positions on the poverty index of the United Nations Development Agency with some of the most outrageous statistics on growth and development. Resource exploitation by multinationals and state corruption of the local governing elites in West Africa deprived all of the countries in the region of the required revenue for national economic and social development. The national economies of these countries have been perpetually shackled for decades with rising digits of huge debt overhangs from the World Bank and the IMF. While the greater proportion of the West African population continues to wallow in unspeakable poverty, the national political elites, on the other hand, have grown unbelievably wealthy through their incestuous relationship with multinational corporate giants.

The three Ebola affected countries in West Africa possessed some of the world's most deplorable health statistics even before the outbreak. Their figures on health care, education, human development, agriculture, and social service delivery in general, have all remained abysmally alarming for decades. Around the time of the outbreak, a health ministry official in Sierra Leone told journalists that the country had only five ambulances – very old ones – for a population of six million people. The high indices of infant and maternal mortality rates are evidence of the dilapidated nature of the health infrastructure in Sierra Leone. Statistical reports have recorded that three of every five pregnant women in Sierra Leone, for instance, die during childbirth[21].

Communities in Sierra Leone continually witness the transformation of poor political party organizers into millionaires who build several mansions each time their party assumes power. They have given up trusting ruling party officials when it comes to caring for their communities. The majority of Sierra Leoneans already held disillusionment with Koroma and his officials before the Ebola outbreak. The questionable circumstances through which Koroma assumed power in the elections of 2007 and 2012 and the authoritarian methods he applied to consolidate power sharply polarized the political landscape of the country. The political credibility of the Koroma regime began nose-diving since he took office. The moral ability of the regime to mobilize national efforts to contain epidemics and

---

[21] There are no specific health statistics on Sierra Leone's infant and maternal mortality figures. While official records from the government of Sierra Leone report that one in eight pregnant women die during childbirth, the WHO and other UN agencies have reported different higher figures. In 2011, when the free-healthcare program for pregnant women and children under five was announced, Amnesty International and other independent organizations stated that three of every five pregnant women risk death during childbirth. Regardless of the statistics, the discordance in figures indicates the prevalent nature of maternal and infant deaths. Nonetheless, there is an agreement that the country ranked top among the worst cases of maternal and infant deaths in the world.

disasters was clearly absent. The reports on theft of Ebola funds and the inflation of health workers lists, which accompanied the national response, underlined the deep rooted nature of graft and state corruption that surrounds the governing elite in the Koroma administration.

In the middle of the chaotic and inadequate response to the Ebola crisis, the Koroma administration's draconian measures were directed not against those who were stealing Ebola funds and hindering the battle against the virus but against ordinary citizens. The state of emergency Koroma proclaimed provided more room for bribery and corruption to flourish. Stories of police abuse at checkpoints and quarantined homes abounded. Health officials received bribes in exchange for travel passes to Ebola hot spots. Newspapers reported stories of humanitarian workers diverting food aid and of public officials pilfering donated funds. These and similar scandals made it clear that the spreading Ebola epidemic was a tragedy on more than one level. The crisis paved the way for deaths, tears, theft, violence, corruption, and for state terror and repression. The ensuing state of emergency imposed by the president turned the country into a dictator's paradise. People watched as the number of deaths and infections continued to climb despite the "robust military measures" assumed by the government.

Koroma himself was aware that corrupt government officials saw the epidemic as a money making project. In a few public statements, he issued vain threats against those suspected of any involvement with stolen Ebola funds. These statements, it appeared, were directed only for the comfort of the local and international press. For Koroma, the country was now a battlefield, a place under siege by the Ebola epidemic. He chose to deal with the situation in a military way. After all, all western nations involved in the fight against Ebola in West Africa also deployed foreign troops into the affected countries.

This book is an independent account of the 2014 Ebola outbreak in West Africa. It is in response to the various explanations advanced by numerous western scientists, academics, and media around the actual origins of the Ebola virus, its mode of transmission, and the actual cause(s) of the explosive nature of the outbreak. At the forefront of the competing but often similar western narratives around the origins of the Ebola epidemic in West Africa is the report by the Robert Koch Institute of Berlin titled "The Zoonotic Origins of the West Africa Ebola Virus." This report offered the foundational scientific story that constitutes the basis for the current narrative that dominates western academic and media discourse on West Africa's Ebola outbreak (the largest health pandemic in recent epidemiological history.)

The German scientist Fabian Leendertz led this report, which was produced by a team of veterinarians, ecologists, epidemiologists, and an anthropologist, all drawn from various institutions in Germany. The team of scientists reportedly travelled to West Africa to investigate "the animal origins of the epidemic" during the first months of the outbreak. Leendertz and his team claimed that West Africa's Ebola epidemic stemmed from "a single zoonotic transmission event" involving a two-year old boy in a village in Guinea who was allegedly infected by hunting or playing with "insectivorous free-tailed bats" living in a nearby hollow tree. The data contained in this report was published on December 30, 2014, in the January 2015 Issue of the *EMBO Molecular Medicine Journal*, and eventually serialized by all major western news agencies.[22] It identified the index case of the virus to have occurred on December 6, 2013, in Miliandou, in southern Guinea. The importance of the Leendertz report to understanding the dominant narrative on the origins of the 2014 West Africa Ebola epidemic is analogous to the importance of Robert Kaplan's 1994 report, "The Coming Anarchy," for Western theorization on the 1990's West African civil wars.

Kaplan's narrative on the unfolding wars in West Africa, published in the *Atlantic Monthly* in February 1994, started off with the criminalization of African cultural behavior.[23] "Crime is what makes West Africa a natural point of departure for my report on what the political character of our planet is likely to be in the twenty-first century," Kaplan wrote. In the introductory sentences Kaplan describes West Africa as "the symbol of worldwide demographic, environmental, and societal stress, in which criminal activity emerges as the real strategic danger. Disease, overpopulation, unprovoked crime, scarcity of resources...are most tellingly demonstrated through a West African prism." This article would become the starting point for almost all-western literature that emerged on the conflicts in West Africa. For many years, Kaplan's report on the West African civil wars of the 1990s became the official narrative on the unfolding catastrophe that accompanied the crisis and conflict situations in the region. Until indigenous African scholars produced literature that offered a different perspective on the conflicts, Kaplan's deliberate location of the wars and instability of West Africa within the realms of environmental concerns, African cultural behavior, and the backwardness of African society, gained monumental credibility among western scholars and leading policy makers.

How true is the "zoonotic transmission" story? Can it actually help us to truly understand the human catastrophe that took place in West Africa? Is there a different narrative on the origin of the Ebola epidemic outside of the Euro-American analysis that now dominates global understandings of the origin of the virus and its mode of transmission? In the case of the Ebola epidemic, Leendertz and his team have applied a Eurocentric theoretical conceptualization of West

[22] Fabian H Leendertz, et al., "Investigating the Zoonotic Origin of the West African Ebola Epidemic," *EMBO Molecular Medicine*, January 2015 (embomolmed.embopress.org/content/early/2014/12/29/emmm.201404792).

[23] See Robert Kaplan's, "The Coming Anarchy" published by the *Atlantic Monthly* in February 1994. Kaplan further advanced this position in Part 1 of his book, *The Ends of the Earth* (1997). Reports stated that Kaplan's article, "The Coming Anarchy" was faxed to every United States embassy in the world when it first appeared in the *Atlantic Monthly*.

Africa to arrive at the "zoonotic transmission story" for the West Africa Ebola virus, similar to what Kaplan did in his 1994 article.

This book's objective is to interrogate the dominant narrative around the origin of the virus, both in terms of place and time, as put forward by Leendertz and his team. In doing so, I examine both the theoretical and empirical evidence provided by Leendertz in his report on the so-called "animal origins" of the virus and show how both Leendertz and Kaplan's reports on war and disease in West African society fall within the usual Eurocentric views and analysis of African culture and civilization. Such narratives, I argue, do not only affect our understanding of the actual causes and gravity of the problems of West African society today, but they often help to criminalize and stigmatize the victims of the violent tragedies themselves.

Leendertz's "zoonotic transmission" narrative, for example, is a direct attack on the cultural behavior of African people vis-à-vis the appetite for eating wild animals and birds as the source of his or her predicament. This analysis is highly influenced by centuries old European beliefs in the primitivism of African people in forested areas. A greater flaw in Kaplan and Leendertz studies is their failure to examine the colonial history of West Africa and its relationship to the underdevelopment of the communities recently affected by war and Ebola; they fail to consider the role of multinational corporate interests and the support of western nations for the various criminal regimes in the region. West Africa's neocolonial subjugation to the West negatively affects the region's economic and social developments, human rights, civil liberties, and democratization, factors which all play key roles in the deadly Ebola epidemic.

The often prejudiced and deliberately abrupt nature of Euro-American interpretations of West Africa as the backyard of the world – a place of poverty, hopelessness, and barbarism – completely ignores the colonial historical realities that continually create the basis for all the crises, wars, conflicts and diseases in the region at least from 1989 (the year West Africa's conflicts of the 1990s began in Liberia with the insurgency of Charles Taylor) to the present. In the case of the Ebola epidemic, a major inadequacy of these Euro-American assertions have been the inability to address fundamental questions relating to the objective reality of the geographical and demographical arrangements of the area. What were the objective conditions in Sierra Leone, Liberia, and Guinea before the outbreak? Why has the Ebola outbreak occurred within the same geographical space where some of West Africa's most brutal civil wars of the 1990s were fought? How do we understand the huge presence of large-scale multinational corporations like Firestone (Liberia), Rio Tinto (Guinea), and African Minerals (Sierra Leone) and their relationship to the persistent territorial underdevelopment of West Africa and the growing instability in the region? And most importantly, why was the international "humanitarian response" very slow and mainly backed by military deployments? To what extent did the existing politics of state repression and corruption often hinder national responses to crises – both war and disease?

It is the answers to these questions that constitute the focus and content of this book. The first part of the book contextualizes West Africa's Ebola outbreak through a historical perspective of viral epidemiology in Africa. This historical contextualization of viral epidemiology examines the deceptive nature of the Robert Koch Institute's 2014 Report by Leendertz and his team of scientists on West Africa's Ebola epidemic. Through an examination of the scientific deception of the Leendertz report, I highlight the direct and indirect efforts by some sections of the western scientific community and its media representatives to cover-up the actual chain of event(s) that resulted in the greatest medical catastrophe in the recent history of global epidemiology. I then proceed to deepen this argument with a further historical examination of the role of the centuries old tradition of western medical experimentation in Africa from the periods of slavery to colonialism and its relationship to epidemiology on the continent. This historical examination challenges both the dominant theoretical and empirical arguments put forward by western scientists in support of the "zoonotic origin" of the Ebola virus in West Africa and its mode of transmission. I then present a counter narrative that situates the origin of the Ebola epidemic outside the parameters of the "zoonotic transmission" story both in terms of place and time.

In the second part of the book, I look at the political economy of the West African Ebola outbreak. In this section, I address the contradictions of international humanitarianism, how autocratic regimes utilize natural disasters to execute dictatorial policies and the relationship between colonial conquest (the contemporary scramble for Africa's resources) and third world epidemiology (the 2014 outbreak). Here I argue that the explosive nature of the virus can be blamed squarely on the international and national response mechanisms. The political leaders of the three affected countries share a common political characteristic: they all came to power through electoral processes whose outcomes were challenged. And the military measures adopted in some of the affected countries, particularly Sierra Leone, were not actually aimed at containing an actual chain of transmission but were instead principally designed to constrict democratic right and national discourse on the origin of the epidemic.

The final part of the book examines the social and economic ramifications of the Ebola epidemic from community to national levels. I examine the questions of human rights, justice, and cultural behavior in West Africa and the long ranging impacts the Ebola epidemic has had upon long established societal norms and traditions in the region. I conclude by arguing that the 2014 Ebola outbreak must be investigated by an internationally established independent panel of forensic experts to help the people of West Africa establish the truth around what actually took place in their communities. Such an investigation, I suggest, must include a pathological and forensic examination of the remains of individuals who are confirmed to have died of Ebola during the outbreak. Independent testimonies of victims and so-called Ebola survivors must be incorporated as part of a process to determine the possible merit of a case for medical genocide against certain individuals and groups who may have participated or condoned the emergence and widespread transmission of the Ebola virus in West Africa. The so-called Marshall plan of the IMF/World Bank's post-Ebola recovery agenda for the affected countries must be substituted for an international program of reparations to the families and communities who suffered irreparable damages due to the outbreak.

PART ONE
Contextualizing West Africa's Ebola Epidemic

CHAPTER 1

WEST AFRICA'S EBOLA OUTBREAK: A QUESTIONABLE NARRATIVE

The severe Ebola virus disease epidemic occurring in West Africa stems from a single zoonotic transmission event to a two-year-old boy in Meliandou, Guinea. We investigated the zoonotic origins of the epidemic using wildlife surveys, interviews, and molecular analyses of bat and environmental samples. We found no evidence for a concurrent outbreak in larger wildlife. Exposure to fruit bats is common in the region, but the index case may have been infected by playing in a hollow tree housing a colony of insectivorous free tailed bats ...

         – Robert Koch Institute[24]

The above excerpt is from the introductory sentences of a report titled "Investigating the Zoonotic Origins of the West African Ebola Epidemic" released by the Robert Koch Institute of Berlin in Germany. The report, published on December 30, 2014, by the European Molecular Biology Organization's (EMBO) *Molecular Medicine Journal*, was the result of research undertaken by a group of predominantly German scientists drawn from several institutions in Germany. The group was headed by Fabian Leendertz, a leading virologist and expert in wildlife epidemiology. At the time of the investigation, Leendertz served as head of the Robert Koch Institute's Research Group on "Epidemiology of Highly Pathogenic Microorganisms."

Leendertz and his team reportedly travelled to West Africa in April of 2014 after the World Health Organization (WHO) formally announced that the *Zaire Ebola virus* (one of five known species of Ebola) was responsible for a number of deaths in southeastern Guinea. The objective of the scientists' trip, according to

---

[24] See the Robert Koch Institute's (RKI) report on 'Investigating the Zoonotic Origin of the West Africa Ebola Epidemic," *EMBO Molecular Medicine* 7 no. 1, (January 2015).

Fabian Leendertz, was to investigate "whether there was a larger Ebola virus outbreak happening in wildlife in the region and how the index case might have gotten infected and sparked the epidemic that spread into other areas of Guinea and then Sierra Leone and Liberia, representing the largest ever recorded outbreak."

Previous Ebola outbreaks in Central Africa in the 1970s reportedly occurred in areas where overwhelming evidence of major wildlife deaths took place. Previous scientific research concluded that hunters in those regions had been exposed to dead animals, contracting the virus by handling and consuming the carcasses they found in the forests of the regions.[25] In the case of West Africa, Leendertz and his team tried to apply the same research templates previously used in the Central African region to identify the origins of the virus. They wanted to establish how animal hunting and eating caused the emergence of the Ebola virus in West Africa and how this consumption of bushmeat led to Ebola's infectious transmission chains.[26]

Leendertz's team focused on the area around a small Guinean village named Meliandou, where supposedly the virus first transferred from a bat to a two-year-old boy by the name of Emile Ouamouno. But West Africa, even according to Leendertz, is a departure from the usual western scientific script on the history of Ebola epidemiology in Africa. Leendertz and his team wrote in the introduction to "The Zoonotic Origin of the West African Ebola Epidemic" that, "The monitoring team did not encounter any wildlife carcasses in their surveys, nor did they document a recent decline in wildlife densities in the region. This suggested that there was likely no amplifying epidemic in wildlife in the region, which could have enabled the virus to jump into the human population."

Leendertz's team continued, "Our surveys of the remaining large mammals in the only two protected areas in proximity to Meliandou suggest they have not experienced a major decline; in fact, carnivore and chimpanzee populations may have increased." Leendertz also added that regional authorities, hunters, and women of the "indexed village" stated that primates are rare in southeastern Guinea and that the few that remain are difficult to hunt. This situation ultimately removed the possibility that the Ebola epidemic, then at its preliminary stages in the region, was caused by the same type of animal-to-human transmission as occurred in the Congo in the 1970s, which were characterized by large wildlife die off and hunter exposure to carcasses of large mammals.

The epidemiological outbreak in West Africa represented a stark contrast with scientific observations supposedly made during previous Ebola epidemiological

---

[25] Walsh and Haseeb, "The Landscape Configuration of Zoonotic Transmission of Ebola Virus Disease in West and Central Africa: Interaction Between Population Density and Vegetation Cover," *PeerJ* 3, no. 735 (2015).

[26] See the RKI's report, "Investigating the Zoonotic Origins of the West African Ebola Epidemic," *EMBO Molecular Medicine* 7 no. 1 (January 2015).

outbreaks in other parts of Africa where the heavy death tolls of wild apes were reported and where scientific claims of a zoonotic origin were easily established. Nonetheless, Leendertz and his team arrived at the conclusions that the 2014 West African Ebola epidemic was the result of a "zoonotic transmission," despite their research findings departing from the historical western scientific script that characterized all Ebola epidemiological origins in other parts of Africa. And, most importantly, they subscribed to the assumption (reported by the Koch Institute as first made aware to them by unidentified "local health officials") that a two-year old boy in Miliandou was the index case of the virus. Even a cursory reading of the report reveals significant unsubstantiated claims and inconsistent evidence of the identity of the index case and of a zoonotic transmission. In fact, the team reports that they found no evidence of Ebola amongst the local wildlife populations.[27]

Nonetheless, to try and get around the problematic lack of a corresponding wildlife die off, Leendertz's team posited that bats were the reservoir for the Ebola virus in West Africa. They based this assumption off the fact that "some fruit and insectivorous bats have been shown to survive experimental Ebola virus infections." This simple fact leads to grand and irresponsible conclusions: "This suggests direct infection by bats is plausible, given that bats, especially fruit bats, are frequently hunted and consumed as bush meat," the report states.

It appears, from Leendertz's own account, that the German scientists forcefully implanted an originating narrative that is born out of a historical western conceptualization of African disease epidemiology to explain the origins of the 2014 Ebola outbreak. To establish this position, the zoonotic transmission story, Leendertz further reported that his team (which consisted of a single anthropologist) conducted additional detailed observations of communal people's behavioral patterns in Meliandou for a little over a week, and they discovered an entrenched tradition of hunting and eating bats. "We found a large tree stump situated approximately fifty meters from the home of the index case near an often-used path leading to a small river used by women for washing. Villagers reported that children used to play frequently in this hollow tree," Leendertz and his team said, adding that, oddly, the tree had been burnt down on March 24, 2014, just a few days prior to their arrival.

Leendertz claimed villagers "reported that once the tree caught fire, a rain of bats started and a large number of bats were collected for consumption. The bats were described as *lolibelo*, that is, small, smelly bats with a long tail." Leendertz concluded that although there was no evidence of additional Ebola infections stemming from the consumption of these bats, the fact that children in Miliandou are said to have regularly caught and played with bats from the tree was proof that

---

[27] Also reflected in Robert Koch Institute's report, "Investigating the Zoonotic Origins of the West African Ebola Epidemic," *EMBO Molecular Medicine* 7 no. 1 (January 2015).

the virus likely emerged out of the insectivorous free-tailed bats from the burnt tree. It is this circumstantial evidence that was used to identify the index case as the two-year old boy that died on December 6, 2013. "Under the assumption that the two-year-old boy was indeed the index case, a source of infection unrelated to food items consumed in the home might be more plausible," Leendertz claimed in a poor attempt to explain the child being the only initial infection. "The close proximity of a hollow tree housing a large colony of free-tailed insectivorous bats, of a species for which serological evidence also suggests Ebola virus, provided opportunity for infection," the team asserted.

It is clear that Leendertz and his team were completely unable to establish any clear relationship between wildlife conditions and the epidemic, nor were they able to establish the presence of the Ebola virus in any of the nearly two-hundred bats they captured in the region. The remains of bat samples taken out of the burnt tree in Miliandou, where the index case is said to have emerged, also failed to show any trace of the Ebola virus. However, Leendertz proceeded with the above conclusion, not as the result of clinical evidence, but deduced supposedly from observation of communal behavioral patterns in the village of Miliandou and the circumstantial coincidence that fruit bats, commonly suspected as reservoirs of the Ebola virus, are hunted for their meat in the southern forest regions of Guinea.

It is the conclusion in this report that still serves as the official western scientific explanation dominating the causative events responsible for the largest Ebola outbreak in recent epidemiological history. This conclusion presents a large scientific dilemma, the result of a preconceived Euro-American notion of disease and crisis in African communities. It is evident that Leendertz and his colleagues' deliberate insistence on establishing the same causative factors for the West African epidemic as the epidemics in the Central African region in the 1970s ignored all of the specificity of geography, ethnography, and demographic variations between and among the various regions of Africa. Their methodological approach to the investigation in Guinea, arriving with a dictated script, failed to consider the specificities of the region they were investigating.

The landscape of the Congo basin and its population dynamics in the 1970s were completely dissimilar from the Mano River enclaves of Guinea, where the 2014 Ebola epidemic is said to have germinated and developed its first migratory chains of infections. Meliandou, for instance, is a small village of thirty-one houses, surrounded by farmland and few large trees. "The landscape in that region is heavily human-modified, with Meliandou surrounded by plantations and bush land rather than tropical rainforests, as was the case for index villages in many previous Zaire Ebola virus outbreaks," the Koch Institute acknowledged. Indeed, Meliandou is not located in a densely forested area like the communities of the Congo basin where the first Ebola epidemic reportedly erupted in the 1970s.

Though bat hunting is a common practice in the southern region of Guinea, in Miliandou and the six other villages studied by the scientists, only adult men reportedly engage in the hunting of fruit bats[28] (as opposed to the insectivorous bats the team claimed as the reservoir of the virus) for meat during the course of the year. This practice itself has existed in Guinea's southern forest region for decades, or even centuries, without any adverse consequences on the life and living patterns of the communities in the region. Even with bat hunting as a habitual practice within the indexed village and the surrounding communities, Leendertz and his team found no evidence that the so-called "animal origins" of the epidemic resulted from any animal or bird hunting practices. If the hunting of bats had been the cause of transmission, the index case of the virus would probably have been located in the adult hunter population.

The fact that the scientists, without establishing the presence of the Ebola virus in either the region's bat or animal populations, still proceeded to confirm a "zoonotic transmission event" involving a two-year old boy as the index case of the virus should raise concern. The conclusion of Leendertz and his team was, therefore, not based on any real clinical examination and investigation that proved beyond all reasonable doubt that the 2014 Ebola epidemic actually originated from a "zoonotic transmission event." This being the case, why has the zoonotic transmission story persisted as the dominating official narrative around the origin of the West African Ebola epidemic?

Historical Context of the Leendertz Narrative

The findings of the Robert Koch Institute's report, conducted early April of 2014, were published on December 30, 2014, at the highest peak of deaths and infections in all three of the most-affected countries in the region: Sierra Leone, Liberia, and Guinea. Since its publication, there has never been any serious discussion on the validity of the findings and the substantive nature of the evidence that led Fabian Leendertz and his team to arrive at the conclusion that the 2014 Ebola epidemic in West Africa originated from a zoonotic transmission event. The Leendertz report has been uncritically accepted as an accurate description of the origin of the virus by nearly all governmental and journalistic institutions involved in the response.

The western media and its academic community overwhelmingly accepted all of the claims of the report without a challenge. The findings and conclusions of the Leendertz report dominated western media coverage and academic discourse on the Ebola epidemic in West Africa months ahead of its formal publication. In an article reporting the contents of the Leendertz report, the *BBC* hailed the Robert Koch Institute's report as "the closest explanation that has been advanced

---

[28] Interviews of villagers in Miliandou reported by Fabian Leendertz and team in the RKI report: "Zoonotic Origins of the West African Ebola Epidemic," *EMBO Molecular Medicine* 7 no. 1 (January 2015).

so far."[29]

The African intellectual community and the African media, in particular, failed to instigate a dialogue or discourse that sought to investigate, examine, or challenge the validity of the assertions and claims advanced in "The Zoonotic Origins of the West African Ebola Epidemic." A greater segment of the African academic community and the African media appeared to have accepted the western narrative as authoritative on the origins of the epidemic regardless of the clear absence of clinical evidence justifying the supposed scientific claims of the report.

In the Mano River countries themselves, the lack of investigation can be attributed in part to the repressive nature of national responses by the regional political elites in West Africa and the brutal enactment of draconian legislation and disease-control mechanisms in response to the epidemic. These repressive and authoritarian responses undermined the existence of the required space that would have encouraged the emergence of a platform necessary for intellectual discourse in response to the analysis from western academics and scientists regarding the 2014 outbreak.

In Sierra Leone, for example, at the time of the publication of the Leendertz report, a two-week national lockdown of the country, ahead of the usual Christmas and New Year celebrations, was already *en force* as part of the robust measures announced by president Ernest Koroma to prevent public gatherings. National emergency regulations, which also outlawed critical debates around the epidemic, did not enhance an open discussion on the developments that were unfolding alongside the Ebola epidemic.[30] This situation largely accounted for the lack of any alternative analysis or comprehensive examination of the contents and claims advanced by Fabian Leendertz and his team regarding the zoonotic transmission story.

But why have the broader western and African intellectual communities and the western and African media failed to examine Leendertz's zoonotic transmission story? The obvious lack of justifiable evidence to credibly support Leendertz's "zoonotic transmission narrative" ultimately means that there must be a different narrative on the origin of the Ebola epidemic, necessarily existing outside of the Euro-American analysis that now dominates global understandings of the origin of the virus and its modes of transmission. It is only such an alternative narrative that will properly explain the objective conditions that created the outbreak and the agency for its widespread transmission. This new, contextualized search for an accurate description of the outbreak and its ramifications must, as

---

[29] Michelle Roberts, "First Ebola Boy Likely Infected by Playing in Bat Tree," *BBC Online*, December 30, 2014 (www.bbc.com/news/health-30632453).

[30] See 'Somber Christmas as Sierra Leone Orders Ebola Lockdown," *AFP*, December 25, 2014, (www.france24.com/en/20141225-sierra-leone-north-under-five-day-ebola-lockdown). Also see "Sierra Leone Cancels Christmas to Reflect on Ebola," *AFP*, December 12, 2014 (www.france24.com/en/20141212-sierra-leone-cancels-christmas-reflect-ebola).

a starting point, situate Fabian Leendertz and his team's report within the general Eurocentric theoretical conceptualization of West Africa when it comes to conflict theory and crisis reporting and analysis.

Analyzing the report and the outbreak within the historical contexts of the socio-cultural, economic, and political factors that produced the outbreak will help to interrogate the validity of the assertions and claims advanced by the Robert Koch Institute's report by Leendertz and his team. It will also equally contextualize the motivational platform from which this team of western scientists built their narrative and help illustrate why the western media continues to participate in the validation of the narrative despite its problematic claims.

This task requires an examination of the historical and professional background of both Fabian Leendertz and the Robert Koch Institute in particular. It also requires an evaluation of the findings recorded in the report itself compared with the actual and prevailing socio-cultural dynamics of everyday life in the West African area where the virus is reported to have originated. An examination of the historical background of the Robert Koch Institute together with an academic scrutiny of the professional scientific work of its most prominent research scientist, Fabian Leendertz, will help to unravel the supposed scientific background which informed the zoonotic transmission narrative and explain how, when subjected to a clinical social diagnosis, the Leendertz narrative does not offer a satisfactory explanation for the origin of the West African Ebola virus.

The Robert Koch Institute, one of Europe's leading epidemiological scientific organizations, named after the prominent German scientist, Robert Heinrich Herman Koch, a celebrated German physician and pioneering microbiologist, is today one of the leading western institutions in the field of epidemiology and virology.[31] Robert Koch, who founded the institute, was a contemporary of Freidrich Ratzel and Eugene Fischer, Germany's leading race scientists in the early-to-mid-twentieth century Europe. Whereas Ratzel was known for creating the theory of *Lebensraum* and Fischer for his role in German eugenic studies, Robert Koch was known for his breakthroughs in the field of bacteriology.[32]

Koch reportedly played a key role in western medical science by identifying the causative agents of tuberculosis, cholera, and anthrax and for giving experimental support to the concept of infectious disease. Koch is regarded as one of Europe's greatest authorities in the area of public health, and it was he who postulated the four generalized principles that linked specific microorganisms to specific diseases, a key advancement in the study of microbiology. As a result

---

[31] See Robert Koch Institute, "The Heirs to Robert Koch," *Protecting Health, Assessing Risks*, PP. 10-11. See also Amsterdamska, Olga, *"Bacteriology, Historical," International Encyclopedia of Public Health*, 2008. Web.

[32] Robert Koch, *"World of Microbiology and Immunology,"* ed. Brenda Wilmoth Lerner and K. Lee Lerner, (Detroit: Biography in Context, 2006) Web. 14 Apr. 2013.
Also see Metchnikoff, Elie, *The Founders of Modern Medicine: Pasteur, Koch, Lister*. (Delanco: Classics of Medicine Library, 2006).

of his groundbreaking research on tuberculosis, Koch was awarded the Nobel Prize in Medicine in 1905.[33] Around this same time, German scientists, including Eugene Fischer, were carrying out experimental studies on the human remains of African victims from the German genocide in Namibia under the auspices of the Kaiser Wilhelm Institute.[34] Like Fischer, Koch was also hugely instrumental in the history of German medical experimentation that occurred from the early-to-mid-twentieth century. His groundbreaking advancements in the field of epidemiology were accomplished through research and experimental studies in Africa and Asia. The Koch Institute, which he founded, continued the tradition of medical research into the 1940s during the German genocide of the Jews. The Robert Koch Institute was directly involved in setting up experiments into typhus vaccines at the Buchenwald Concentration Camp during the Holocaust; the experiments killed 127 of the 537 camp inmates that were used as human subjects for its research.[35]

Recounting the nature of the experiment, historian Richard Evans noted in his book, *The Third Reich at War,* that "after being approved on 29 December 1941 at a meeting of representatives of various interested parties, including the Army Sanitary Inspectorate, the Military SS, the Reich Health Leader and the Robert Koch Institute (the leading center for bacteriological research), experiments were set in motion at the Buchenwald concentration camp. In the initial experiment, one hundred and forty-five inmates were first given a course of injections of the vaccine...and a fortnight or so after the final dose, injected again, this time with the blood of a patient infected with the most virulent form of typhus. The experiment was repeated a further eight times with different vaccines. For one hundred and twenty-seven out of the five hundred and thirty-seven camp inmates subjected to these procedures the results were fatal..."[36]

The Robert Koch Institute, like the Kaiser Wilhelm Institute, carried out the same human medical experimentation in continuation of the work of its founder. Historical records from that era indicated that prisoners from all over Europe and the Soviet Union which included Jews, Polish and Slavs, the mentally ill, and the physically disabled from birth defects, were all used as subjects of its research.[37] It is from these studies that the Robert Koch Institute assumed its current leadership

[33] Brock Thomas. *Robert Koch: A life in Medicine and Bacteriology.* (Washington DC: ASM Press, 1999). Also see article by Robert Koch (10 April 1882) "Die Aetiologie der Tuberculose" (The Etiology of Tuberculosis), *Berliner Klinische Wochenschrift* (Berlin Clinical Weekly), vol. 19: pp. 221-230.

[34] Mahmood Mamdani, *When Victims Become Killers: Colonialism, Nativism, and the Genocide in Rwanda.* (Princeton: Princeton University Press, 2001). Also see Olusoga, David and Erichsen, Casper W, *The Kaiser's Holocaust. Germany's Forgotten Genocide and the Colonial Roots of Nazism.* (London: Faber and Faber, 2010).

[35] Naomi Baumslag, *Murderous Medicine: Nazi Doctors, Human Experimentation, and Typhus,* p. 37 (Westport: Praeger Publishers, 2005).

[36] Evans, Richard (2009) *The Third Reich at War,* p. 217-282 (New York: Penguin, 2009).

[37] See pp. 217-282 of Richard Evans, *The Third Reich at War.*

position in the study of epidemiology and viral diseases.

Today, the Robert Koch Institute is one of the central institutions for health protection in Germany. It serves the German Federal Ministry of Health as a central scientific institution in the field of biomedicine. The institute combines risk research with political advice. Its most important tasks include protection against infectious diseases and the analysis of the health situation in Germany. On the international medical environment, the institute is involved in many different works with the European Centre for Disease Prevention and Control (ECDC) and the World Health Organization (WHO) through laboratory work in connection with outbreak investigations.

Fabian Leendertz, a wildlife epidemiologist and evolutionary biologist, is one of the leading scientists at the Robert Koch Institute and the Max Planck Institute for Evolutionary Anthropology in Germany. With over a hundred and twenty-five publications on viral epidemiology and tropical diseases, Leendertz is one of the institute's most widely cited authorities on global epidemiology and infectious diseases. He has conducted research on the "animal origins" of most viruses and has a huge volume of works documenting his findings from the Congo to Sudan to the Ivory Coast, where he reportedly investigated the environmental relationship between epidemiological outbreaks in Africa and African cultural behavior towards the environment.[38]

A year before the Ebola outbreak in West Africa, Fabian Leendertz told the medical journal, *Science in School* that the majority of human pathogens come from elsewhere in the animal kingdom and can now, due to globalizing transportation and technology, spread easily throughout the global human population. "It is far easier for a pathogen to spread between countries today making what would have been a small incident in the past to quickly become a worldwide outbreak," he said, adding that, "pathogens that have recently been transmitted from animals to humans can be particularly dangerous because they are new to the human immune system."[39]

This desire to investigate how new pathogens are being spread from animals to humans and the threat which these transmitted diseases pose for the global health system and its international political order is what actually marked Leendertz's interest in epidemiological studies.[40] This scientific study is called

---

[38] RKI, "The Heirs to Robert Koch," *Protecting Health, Assessing Risks*. See also Julia Heymann, "Evolving Threats: Investigating New Zoonotic Infections," *Science in School*, no. 27 (Autumn 2013): pp. 12-16.

[39] Julia Heymann, "Evolving Threats: Investigating New Zoonotic Infections," *Science in School*, no. 27 (Autumn 2013) pp. 12-16.

[40] Julia Heymann, "Evolving Threats: Investigating New Zoonotic Infections," pp. 12-16. Haymann introduced the article in the following words: "In the African forest, Fabian Leendertz and his team look for new infectious agents that can be transmitted from animals to humans. Could one of them cause the next pandemic?" She asked in the opening sentences of the article published a year before the West African outbreak was reported.

zoonosis; the word is a derivative from the Greek words *zoon* (meaning creature) and *nosos* (referring to a disease). It is used to describe how deadly infectious agents are transmitted between animals and humans. Two established examples of global epidemics that have been traced to this mode of transmission (zoonotic transmission theory) are rabies and the bubonic plague, both of which decimated a huge sector of the European population.

Zoonotic transmission is, therefore, not new to the Robert Koch Institute, which sponsored the investigation on the 2014 Ebola epidemic in West Africa. The zoonotic transmission theory is part of the history of the Koch Institute's evolution as a leading medical research institution in Europe. Robert Koch, the institute's founder and first director, was instrumental in the trends that established the theory of zoonotic studies as a method in determining the origin of major health epidemics or pandemics. It is in continuation of the tradition of Robert Koch that Fabian Leendertz and his team journeyed to the African forests of the Congo, South Sudan, Tanzania, and Ivory Coast looking for new infectious agents that can be transmitted from animals to humans. The urge to investigate new zoonotic infections, according to Leendertz, is to find out if one of these new infectious agents, arising out of a possible zoonotic transmission, could cause the next global health pandemic.

In an Issue of the *Science in School* journal, published a year before the 2014 West African outbreak, Leendertz speculated that wild animals such as fruit bats or monkeys that are hunted for food in Africa could be the next potential source of a global epidemiological outbreak. "The primates include lemurs, monkeys and the great apes, such as chimpanzees and gorillas. Any virus or bacterium that infects our primate relatives could also be dangerous to us," he stated. To identify new infectious agents that jump the species barrier, Leendertz took a team of German research scientists to investigate the forested regions of West Africa beginning in 2004. This research project was conducted in the Ivory Coast in collaboration with behavioral scientists that are part of the Great Ape Health Monitoring Unit, an institute that uses the chimpanzee sanctuary of the Ivory Coast to provide space for researchers from around the world who want to obtain samples from wild apes.[41]

For Leendertz's research project, a team of behavioral scientists was stationed in the Ivory Coast with the task of monitoring all the apes that were being studied. They collected and transported the blood, feces, and urine samples of any ape that fell ill during the course of the study. In an instance where an ape died, the team would perform an autopsy on the corpse of the dead ape and transmit the samples to Fabian Leendertz and his group in Berlin. There, Fabian Leendertz and his team subjected the samples to multiple laboratory experiments to identify

---

[41] See Julia Heymann, "Evolving Threats: Investigating New Zoonotic Infections," pp. 12-16.

the pathogen responsible for the illness and/or death of the apes. The laboratory tests were designed to expose the identity of the microbe by revealing its genome sequence or characteristic surface molecules.

A scientific technique was applied that multiplied DNA sequences and made them easier to identify. After identifying the microorganisms, Leendertz and his team undertook a further task to locate the region(s) unique to certain microorganisms. If one of those specific sequences was present in any of the samples, the pathogen was then identified as belonging to a certain bacterial or viral family. By testing different types of ape samples – blood, feces, or urine – the scientists searched for specific types of diseases, especially those caused by respiratory, intestinal, or systemic pathogens. "If the pathogen was an unknown microorganism, we try to culture it and isolate the whole genome for sequencing. Then we present the newly discovered microbe to the scientific world," Fabian Leendertz explained. Leendertz added that a key focus was to find out if the newly discovered sample virus would infect only apes or if it was transmissible to human beings. The process also examined how a possibly infected person can transmit the pathogen to other members of the human population.

After the studies on the apes, Leendertz and his team of German scientists travelled to West Africa to undertake the next phase of the study. They took samples from people living close to where the sample virus was being tested on the apes. The scientists also worked with local doctors in the region who were sending samples from human tests to Germany for further clinical examinations.

Leendertz and his team wanted to find out how the microbe, when found in human samples acquired either directly from apes or indirectly from another host, might cause an epidemic or even a pandemic. The researchers also tried to establish how the pathogen transmitted from one person to another. Using this data, the researchers hoped to eventually identify the source and the means of transmission of a newly discovered pathogen, in order to investigate how a given pathogen should be handled in the case of an epidemic.

"We carry a mobile miniature lab with which we can instantly test for the most dangerous species, like an Ebola virus," Fabian Leendertz explained. It was through this process that the group announced in 2004 that it discovered how a previously harmless soil bacterium known as *bacillus cereus,* acquired from a related pathogenic bacterium *(bacillus anthracis)*, contained the genetic properties necessary to produce the dangerous anthrax toxin.[42] The bacterial strain that evolved from this genetic transfer was believed to live in the soil and have the ability to become highly virulent (i.e. poisonous, infectious), thereby serving as a lethal threat to chimpanzees. A major goal of the project was to test whether a specific pathogenic strain found in the local human population through animal

---

[42] Fabian Leendertz and Co, "Characterization of Bacillus anthracis-Like Bacteria Isolated from Wild Great Apes from Cote d'Ivoire and Cameroon," *Journal of Bacteriology*, 188, No. 15 (Aug. 2006): pp. 5333–5344.

transmission could be protected by vaccination. In other words, the project was designed to develop vaccines for the anticipated "new zoonotic diseases" which pose a potential threat to global health.

Leendertz has been conducting medical research in Africa for over a decade now. In expanding his zoonotic investigations, he stated that the growth of human residential areas in Africa represented a threat to an encounter with new pathogens. "Changing the local ecosystem eliminates some species, some of which could bring zoonotic microbes with them," he stated. Leendertz added that in parts of Africa, where wild animals are an important food source and rapid population growth has stimulated the bushmeat trade, there are even more risks of zoonotic infections. Fabian Leendertz's research in Africa focused on the possible method of animal to human disease transmission.[43]

This is the scientific background that informs Fabian Leendertz's investigation into the 2014 "animal origins of West Africa's Ebola epidemic." It is obvious that Fabian Leendertz's report deliberately located the origin of the 2014 Ebola epidemic within the realms of environmental concerns and African cultural behavior, by willfully ignoring the obvious historical exploitation and appropriation of the human and environmental resources of West Africa by multinationals and corporate entities for the purpose of medical research and experimentation. This is a deliberate academic amputation of the recent social and economic history of Euro-American conquest and destruction of Africa's vast environmental resources and rich biodiversity for the fulfillment of the twenty-first century ambitions of western medical science. This is, however, a position that is not only born out of willful distortion and deception, but it forms part of the historic role and calculated effort of the western scientific community and its academic intellectuals, of which Leendertz is a member, to provide justification for the ongoing exploitation of Africa's resources (human, material, and environmental resources).

The Criminalization of African Culture: From Kaplan to Leendertz

The Leendertz report, which today forms the basis for the dominant western narrative on the origins of the 2014 West African Ebola epidemic, is not unprecedented. It directly corresponds to famed journalist Robert Kaplan's 1994 report, "The Coming Anarchy," on the unfolding civil wars of West Africa in the 1990s.[44]

Kaplan's article, "The Coming Anarchy" was published in the *Atlantic Monthly* in February of 1994, as the West African civil wars raged. The article started off with the criminalization of African cultural behavior. "Crime is what makes West Africa a natural point of departure for my report on what the political character

---

[43] See RKI's, "The Heirs to Robert Koch," *Protecting Health, Assessing Risks.*

[44] See Robert Kaplan's *"The Coming Anarchy"* and *"The Ends of the Earth"* in the list of bibliography for additional details.

of our planet is likely to be in the twenty-first century," Kaplan wrote. In addition, Kaplan said, "West Africa is becoming the symbol of worldwide demographic, environmental, and societal stress, in which criminal activity emerges as the real strategic danger... Disease, overpopulation, unprovoked crime, scarcity of resources...are most tellingly demonstrated through a West African prism."

Kaplan's narrative later became the starting point for almost all-western literature that emerged on the conflicts in West Africa. For many years, Kaplan's report on the West African civil wars of the 1990s became the official narrative on the unfolding catastrophe that accompanied the crisis and conflict situations in West Africa. Kaplan deliberately located the wars and instability of West Africa within the realms of environmental concerns. The centrality of African cultural behavior and the backwardness of African society to explain human tragedy gained monumental credibility among western scholars and leading policy makers before it was countered by indigenous African scholars whose literature on the wars offered a different perspective and addressed the fundamental questions of the historical grievances that were central to the wars.

Leendertz's theory on the so-called "animal origins" of the West Africa Ebola virus, therefore, falls within this usual Eurocentric view and analysis of African culture and civilization that often locates the African and his or her environment within the perpetual confines of savagery and barbarism requiring the civilizing hand of the European missionary now represented by multitudes of aid workers and military forces. These misconceptions not only affect global understandings of the actual causes and gravity of the problems of African society, but they often criminalize and stigmatize the African victims of colonial aggression and multinational exploitation.

In the case of the 2014 West African Ebola epidemic, Leendertz deliberately and scornfully transformed the village of Miliandou and the family of Emile Ouamouno, the infant who died on December 6, 2013, into global news items and objects of scientific theorizations without any clinical data that conclusively supported his conclusion. Through this dishonest theoretical invention, Leendertz and his colleagues not only criminalized the victims of the medical tragedy, but they intentionally altered the image and reputation of the family, the community, and the millions of other West Africans whose human and environmental space have been invaded by the predatory forces of western medical science.

The zoonotic transmission narrative of Leendertz and his team is not only a misrepresentation of African culture and African civilization, but it absolutely failed to provide a truthful scientific narrative that explains, both theoretically and empirically, the actual origin and real causes of the 2014 West African outbreak. The evidence adduced by Leendertz and his team to provide their "zoonotic transmission narrative" for the West African outbreak absolutely lacks clinical merit and scientific proof, and is seriously flawed. Where and how can the actual origin and causes of the outbreak be located and explained? To better understand the origin of the 2014 outbreak, a historical examination of the development of western medical science and the evolution of viral epidemiology in Africa are essentially required. It is only from a historical examination of the events which preceded the 2014 outbreak and created both the conditions and the agency for its transmission, that the origin of the epidemic can be unraveled. It is also from such an approach that the actual motives of the Robert Koch Institute's report of Leendertz can be fully contextualized and understood.

CHAPTER 2

THE HISTORICAL CONTEXT OF VIRAL EPIDEMICS IN AFRICA

Western medicine has relied on human and animal experimentation since ancient times. It was by dissecting the bodies of criminals and the poor, that Greek physicians discovered the nervous system in 300 B.C. But it was only after the rigorous experimental design called the controlled clinical trials emerged in the 1940s and was codified into U.S. law in 1962 that the global hunt for experimental bodies began in earnest...

— Sonia Shah, The Body Hunters[45]

The utilization of African environmental reservations and forestry habitats for contemporary western medical research and experimentation is widespread across Africa. For several centuries, Africa has served as a site for many western medical research and experimentation efforts. Several of these medical research projects were ongoing in West Africa for many decades before the 2014 outbreak was reported. These experimental studies and scientific research projects are not specific to German institutions, like the Robert Koch Institute, or restricted to the work of German scientists like Fabian Leendertz alone. Across the forest jungles and rural cities of Sierra Leone, Liberia, and Guinea is a conglomeration of huge multinational entities, corporate organizations and leading pharmaceutical corporations carrying out dogged medical research on vaccine development in response to deadly pathogens with a bio-weapons potential against civilian or military targets. These institutions range from western universities, medical

---

[45] Sonia Shah, *The Body Hunters* (New York and London: The New Press, 2006). Sonia Shah recounts how the multinational pharmaceutical industry, in its quest to develop lucrative drugs, exported its clinical research industry to Africa and others of the developing world; mostly places where ethical issues and patients' rights are often violated.

institutions, individual laboratory scientists, and pharmaceutical corporations in the United States and Europe engaged in multiple and diverse medical research projects and joint scientific studies.

The entirety of these activities amounts to millions of dollars in international finance and funding all designed as part of a global program to counter the supposed threat of bio-terrorism in the twenty-first century. These projects are surreptitiously executed in specific West African countries under the cover of "investigating new infectious diseases" or "neglected tropical diseases." In Liberia, for instance, a project that involved leading American scientists from Tulane University and other institutions was carried out at the Liberian Institute for Biomedical Research (LIBR), about sixty-five miles in the forest east of Monrovia. The LIBR, known by American scientists as Vilab II, was established in 1974 as a world-class research facility to develop scientific breakthroughs for a variety of viral infections, including hepatitis and HIV.[46]

At the Vilab II compound, American scientists carried out the most gruesome experimental use of over two hundred chimpanzees in a medical research funded by the New York Blood Center (NYBC). The project, part of an international program for the development of hepatitis vaccines, infected the chimpanzees with hepatitis and river blindness among other diseases, and then used them for several decades in the development of vaccines for the treatment of hepatitis and for an investigation on the HIV/AIDS virus.

For over thirty years Betsy Brotman, a native of Newark employed by the NYBC, ran the laboratory in Monrovia. Brotman left Bennington College in 1968 and took up a secretarial position with the NYBC's research laboratory on East 67th Street in New York. But her desk job did not last long. She was dispatched to West Africa in 1971 to collect blood samples from wild chimpanzees and to investigate whether blood-sucking insects such as bed bugs were transmitting Hepatitis B. In 1974, Brotman was stationed permanently in Liberia where she assembled a colony of chimpanzees for the hepatitis studies and vaccine tests.

"Chimpanzees are well suited for such work because they can carry human hepatitis viruses but unlike their human relations do not develop serious illness," Brotman told the *New York Times* in an article published on July 17, 1984.[47] The NYBC chose Liberia as an ideal location for the experimental study because it was part of the chimpanzee's home range in West Africa. And the then government of Liberia, an ally of the United States, allowed for the biomedical laboratory to be set-up in its territory. At the jungle compound, the chimps live in spacious

---

[46] Andrew C. Revkin, "A Life's Work Disrupted in Liberia: Newark Native Hopes to Return to Her Study of Chimps," *New York Times*, May 1, 1996. (www.nytimes.com/1996/05/01/nyregion/life-s-work-disrupted-liberia-newark-native-hopes-return-her-study-chimps.html). Web. 10 July 10, 2015.

[47] Clifford D. May, "Lab Chimps Prepared for Difficult Retirement in the Wild," *New York Times*, July 17, 1984, (www.nytimes.com/1984/07/17/science/lab-chimps-prepared-for-difficult-retirement-in-the-wild.html), Web. 10 July 2015.

outdoor cages, Brotman said, instead of cramped in small cages inside sealed buildings, as they are in primate centers in the US.

Scientists at the compound made substantial progress in the fight against viral hepatitis. They ran medical experiments on more than one hundred chimps to test out vaccines for hepatitis. The vaccine for Hepatitis B was developed and tested, and methods for eliminating viruses from blood were also said to have been refined there. It is through this research experiment that American scientists were able to unravel the puzzle of Hepatitis C, which afflicted some ten million Americans at the time. The laboratory also worked on a possible vaccine against the parasite that causes river blindness, a disease affecting some seventeen million Africans.

But the chimpanzees who contributed to this research that led to the development of the hepatitis vaccine were all dumped and left abandoned to perish in Farmington Island, forty miles off the coast of Monrovia in Liberia. Farmington Island, popularly known as Monkey Island by Liberians, is now the last destination for over sixty chimpanzee left overs that were used in the NYBC's hepatitis research at the Liberian Institute for Biomedical Research. In 1984, the *New York Times* stated in an article published on July 17, that one-fourth of the chimpanzees used in the hepatitis research became an asymptomatic carrier of the virus, which, therefore, made all the remaining chimpanzees dumped at Farmington Island infectious agents of the virus.

Slavery, Colonialism and Evolution of Western Medicine

However, this history of western medical experimentation in Africa and on African people did not start within the last one hundred years. And it did not begin with the intervention of western medical science in containing and/or controlling recent epidemiological events in Africa within the last five decades. Western medical science, in particular, played a significant role in the European enslavement and colonization of Africa. The advancements that occurred within Western medicine over the last three hundred years (including studies in disease typology and patterns) cannot be divorced from the general history of oppression and exploitation of the African population for land, labor, and environmental resources, which transformed the economic conditions of Europe and North America.

It would have been difficult or even impossible for the Atlantic slave trade to persist without the role of western medical science. Western physicians and slave owners were dependent on each other for the mutual continuation of their trade. The main interests of western medical practitioners in African slaves were twofold: they depended on slavery for both economic gains and for the clinical material for Euro-American medical research. Slavery offered western physicians the human bodies needed for the development of medical research the same way it provided free labor to plantation owners in the Americas. It is from the diverse studies carried out on the body parts of African slaves that the essential growth and development of western medical science can be traced. Before this period, western medical science was in its embryonic stages.

The evolutionary history of western medical science was born out of the same brutal historical circumstances that transformed the economic and social realities of Europe and North America into epicenters of the global market economy. At the heart of conquest and subjugation of African people and African land (from slavery to colonialism) was the search for human and material resources required for the ongoing industrial and scientific developments of Euro-American societies, all to the obvious detriment of African communities. The socio-political and economic processes that are responsible for the hegemonic position of western societies in today's world are not produced by the independent genius of the Euro-American mind. They are the direct result of violence, abuse and, in most instances, carefully executed genocidal programs. It is through war and territorial conquest that western civilization and scientific advancements were born and are being maintained.

Putting this situation into proper historical context, Walter Rodney in his book, *How Europe Underdeveloped Africa*, records that Africa's contribution to European capitalist growth extended over vital sectors such as shipping, insurance, the formation of companies, capitalist agriculture, technology, and the manufacture of machinery. The effects of European expansionist activity on Africa, according to Rodney, are so wide-ranging that many are seldom brought to the attention of the public.[48]

These wide-ranging consequences, which are seldom discussed, include the place of western medical science in aiding the devastating historical encounter between Europe and Africa. The results of this relationship birthed the proceeds which feed medical research in Europe and North America. Alongside the evil crimes of slavery and colonialism are the often under-studied history of western medical science as a key benefactor and an integral component of the centuries of colonial conquest and the development of global capitalism's scientific ideas and theories. Along with the conquest of African land and resources, European conquest entailed the ownership of the bodies of living and dead Africans by western physicians for experimentations and research studies into disease control and cure.

Writing about the significance of the period of Euro-American enslavement of Africans to the historical evolution of western medical science, Harriet A. Washington notes in the book *Medical Apartheid* that the germ theory, which revealed the microbial nature of disease and led to the first grand waves of disease

---

[48] Rodney Walter, *How Europe Underdeveloped Africa* (London: Bogle-L'Ouverture, 1972).

cures, was still unknown prior to the widespread enslavement of Africans. "The existence of pathogens such as bacteria, viruses, and fungi was unsuspected. Almost no effective treatments existed for prevalent diseases until the eighteenth century," she wrote. Washington added that even the simplest public health measures such as hand-washing and antiseptic techniques, clean water, pathogen free housing, untainted food supply, sewage management, and quantitative disease reporting were unknown to western medical science.[49]

In the American context, for example, J. Marion Sims, the founder of the United States first women's hospital and the "father of gynecology," achieved breakthroughs in gynecological surgery through the utilization of African slaves for medical experimentation. Sims perfected his surgical methods on the bodies of African slave women without the use of anesthesia, many of whom he purchased for the sole purpose of medical experimentation.[50] The medical experimentation of Sims extended from African slave women to African children. He is reported to have also openly experimented on many African infants in Alabama.[51]

The medical journals and personal papers of pre-civil war American physicians, especially in the south, contain cold accounts of medical experimentation on Africans, both living and dead. Stephen Kenny, a University of Liverpool expert on human experimentation on African slaves, records that the "history of human experimentation under American slavery calls for a careful systematic or thematic approach that deploys a wider range of available sources, in order to underscore the banality of medical research in the slave South." Kenny stated that "in published medical case histories there are . . . clear traces of southern medical researchers making regular and systematic use of slave patients."[52]

There is massive evidence of medical experimentation on slaves in the Americas, and before the age of informed consent, countless Africans and other vulnerable populations such as the poor, criminals, and immigrants, were used in studies that led to breakthroughs in western medical science.[53] "Restrained and immobilized for many such experiments, with their protests forcibly overridden, slave patients were subject to painful and invasive procedures repeated with great frequency and over extended time-periods, in medical trials that might cause injury, worsen a condition, or even result in death," Kenny noted in his 2015 study

---

[49] Harriet Washington, *Medical Apartheid: The Dark History of Medical Experimentation on Black Americans from Colonial Times to the Present* (New York: Double Day, 2007) p. 20 and pp. 620-621.

[50] Sara Spettel and White, Mark Donald White, "The Portrayal of J. Marion Sims' Controversial Surgical Legacy," *The Journal of Urology*, (2011): pp. 424-427. Accessed June 19, 2015.

[51] S. C. Kenny, "I Can Do The Child No Good': Dr. Sims And The Enslaved Infants Of Montgomery, Alabama," *Social History of Medicine* 20, no. 2 (2007): pp. 223-41.

[52] Stephen C. Kenny, "Power, Opportunism, Racism: Human Experiments under American Slavery," *Endeavour* 39, no. 1 (2015): pp. 10-20.

[53] Stephen C. Kenny, "The Development of Medical Museums in the Antebellum American South: Slave Bodies in Networks of Anatomical Exchange," *Bulletin of the History of Medicine* 87, no. 1 (2013): pp. 32-62.

"Power, Opportunism, Racism: Human Experiments under American Slavery."

The African as fodder for western medical experimentation survives from the time of slavery through the colonial period and into modern time. One example of such incidents is the infamous forty-year-long Tuskegee Syphilis experiment, wherein the United States Public Health Service injected hundreds of rural-African males in Alabama with Syphilis to monitor the progression of the disease from the 1930s to the 1970s.

In other words, the history of epidemiology and the scientific resolution of the complexity of the internal organic arrangement of the human being are directly linked to the medical research and experimentation that occurred alongside other processes during the periods of slavery and colonialism. Colonial aggression was not driven only by a desire for labor or inanimate resources alone – land, minerals, marine and energy resources – but was also driven by a desire for resources necessary for biochemical advancements. Plants, animals, and human beings were also part of the accumulated capital that became integral to the development of western scientific knowledge, which produced not only disease cures but also the thoughts that advanced racial justifications for the evils of slavery and colonial conquest.

Western medical scientists shared the common interests of the economic and political classes of Europe and America, and they advanced scientific justifications for the ideas of the racial inferiority of African people to white people, which justified the crimes of slavery and colonialism. An examination of all the leading medical literature from the eighteenth century onwards reveals a shocking amount of evidence of the energy devoted by western medical scientists in advancing scientific arguments in favor of the superiority of white people over blacks. This examination also exposes how the morphological features of African people justified their utilization as human objects for the production of the intellectual and material needs of the evolving capitalist economy. More examples from the United States, for instance, include scientists like Josiah Clark Nott, Samuel George Morton, Louis Agassiz, and George Robins, all prominent members of the American school of ethnology who played a significant role in defending slavery by portraying the enslaved blacks as inherently debased.[54] They argued that no amount of training, education, or good treatment could make African people equal to whites.

In his book *Crania Americana,* published in 1839, Samuel Morton stated that physical differences between blacks and whites suggested a hierarchy of humanity. Morton arrived at this conclusion after his supposed study of how the differences

---

[54] Josiah Clark Nott, et al. "Types of Mankind: Or, Ethnological Researches : Based Upon the Ancient Monuments, Paintings, Sculptures, and Crania of Races, and Upon Their Natural, Geographical, Philological and Biblical History," Illustrated by Selections from the Inedited Papers of Samuel George Morton and by Additional Contributions from L. Agassiz, W. Usher, and H.S. Patterson (1854). See also, Josiah Clark Nott et al., *Indigenous Races of the Earth; Or, New Chapters of Ethnological Inquiry; Including Monographs on Special Departments* (1857).

in the human skull measurements of Africans from Europeans were indicative of a hierarchy of racial typology.[55] Morton claimed that the largeness of the European's skull represented the mass character of his/her brains, whereas the tiny nature of the skull of the African represented the miniscule nature of his/her brain. It was from Morton that the science of phrenology, a method used to determine human behavior and intelligence through the size of the skull, was said to have developed.

Other western scientists, such as Samuel Cartwright and Josiah Nott, advanced Morton's ideas on race and the inferiority of Africans to Europeans in subsequent scholarly works. Cartwright and Nott offered justifications for the enslavement and colonization of Africans and the abusive use of their body parts for the advancement of medical studies on disease control and cure. Cartwright, in particular, made a household name for himself out of his theological and scientific arguments on the racial superiority of Caucasians. In 1848 Cartwright noted in his famous thesis, *The Disease and Physical Peculiarities of the Negro Race*,[56] that "blacks' physical and mental defects made it impossible for them to survive without white supervision." He claimed that the cranium of blacks was ten percent smaller than that of whites, which he said prevented the full development of the brain and caused a stunting of the intellect. It was Cartwright who enforced the notion that the differences in the body features of whites and blacks suggest that, "the same medical treatment which would benefit or cure a white man would often injure or kill a Negro." He supported his claims with a description of a list of imaginary black diseases and argued that African protests against brutal slave labor treatments on the plantations represented a behavioral anomaly that should be cured with corporal punishments or quarantines. "Put the patient to some hard kind of work in the open air and sunshine...making the slothful negro take exercise, puts into active play the lungs, through whose agency the vitalized blood is sent to the brain to give liberty to the mind," Cartwright advocated in the *Southern Medical Report* in 1850.[57]

It was out of Cartwright's essays that the universal belief in the existence of uniquely African or black diseases gained monumental recognition, eventually leading to a call from western medical and political leaders for the typological identification and differentiation of diseases along racial and regional boundaries. Following Cartwright's "Report on the Disease and Physical Peculiarities of the Negro Race," another popular work enforcing Cartwright's arguments appeared entitled *Types of Mankind*, jointly written in 1854 by Josiah Nott and George

---

[55] Samuel George Morton, *Crania Americana; or, A Comparative View of the Skulls of Various Aboriginal Nations of North and South America: To which is Prefixed An Essay on the Varieties of the Human Species* (Philadelphia: J. Dobson, 1839).

[56] Samuel Cartwright, "Report on the Diseases and Physical Peculiarities of the Negro Race," *DeBow's Review* XI, (1851), Web 4 Oct. 2007.

[57] Thomas Roderick Dew, "Defense of Slavery: Theorists of Racial Inequality," *Miami-Dade County Public Schools*, (2011). Archived from the original on July 19, 2011. Web. 21 April 2015.

Gliddon. Also published around the same time of Cartwright's famous report on the peculiar diseases of the African was Thomas Carlyle's pamphlet *Occasional Discourse on the Negro Question,* published in England in 1849.[58] Carlyle's argument was in defense of the cruelty of slavery and was to become a starting point for the scientific theories that were to sweep across Europe ten years later. At the root of these theories of scientific racism was Charles Darwin's *On the Origin of Species,* published in 1859 in England.[59]

At the very heart of Darwin's scientific argument is the belief that evolution proceeds by the survival of the fittest, i.e. survival of individuals who have the necessary phenotypes for survival and reproduction. Survival of the fittest entails mutational differences within a species. Mutations that result in advantages for individuals eventually result in the proliferation of the mutation until genetic drift occurs. Darwin stated that differential survival rates due to specific traits (developed via mutations) produce distinct races (what Darwin identified as sub-species) and eventually new species entirely through a process called speciation.

Though the notion that that sub-species (or races) exist within *Homo sapiens* is not scientifically valid, the application of Darwinism to humans became a preoccupation of the political and economic classes of Europe in the furtherance of their colonial conquest and occupation of foreign territories for land and other natural resources. It was from this Social Darwinism perspective that the scientific ideas, which animated the dark racial history of Nazi Germany and its holocaust against Jews in the 1940s, can be traced.

Scientific Racism, Nazi Germany, and the Herero Genocide

Influential German biologists of the early twentieth century revealed in their writings how Darwin's theory and publications had a major influence upon Nazi race policies. Hitler, in his writings, personally articulated Darwin's ideas of a superior race.[60] Hitler believed that the human gene pool could be improved by using selective breeding, similar to how farmers breed superior cattle strains. Hitler's

---

[58] Thomas Carlyle, *"Occasional Discourse on the Negro Question," Fraser's Magazine,* 1849. Thomas Carlyle is referred to as a Scottish philosopher, satirical writer, essayist, and historian. He is considered one of the most important social commentators in the Victorian era in England. His 1837 book, *The French Revolution: A History* was the source for Charles Dickens' 1859 novel, *A Tale of Two Cities.* Carlyle is said to have coined the term "dismal science" for economics. In mathematics, he is said to have invented the method used in quadratic equations known as the *Carlyle circle* and for also developing ruler-and-compass constructions of regular polygons. Carlyle's philosophical ideas, notably his appreciation of German culture, the Norse mythology and his anti-democratic views, are considered as theoretical prelude to the ideas of fascism.

[59] Charles Darwin, *On the Origin of Species by Means of Natural Selection, or the Preservation of Favored Races in the Struggle for Life* (1st ed.) 1859. Web 24 October 2008.

[60] Philip Thurtle, "The Creation of Genetic Identity,". *SEHR 5 (Supplement: Cultural and Technological Incubations of Fascism),* 17 December 1996, Web. 11 November 2008. See, for another example, Edwards, A. W. F. *The Genetical Theory of Natural Selection* (New York: Oxford, April 2000): pp. 1419–1426, Web. 11 November 2008. Also see John Wilkins, *"Evolving Thoughts: Darwin and the Holocaust 3: Eugenics," Science Blogs,* Web. 11 November 2008.

government relied heavily upon the application of Darwinism to the human and social sphere in the formulation of its racial policies.[61] A central policy of Hitler's administration was the development and implementation of policies designed to protect a "German superior race," which required the prevention of the "inferior races" from mixing with the German race. This "superior race belief" was based on the theory of group inequality within each species, a major presumption and requirement of Darwin's "survival of the fittest theory." It was this philosophy that culminated in the extermination of approximately six million Jews and four million other people who belonged to what German scientists judged "inferior races."

But the systematization of Social Darwinism by the Germans into a policy of extermination did not begin with Hitler and the Jewish holocaust in Germany. Following the Berlin Conference of 1884-85, where the partition of Africa was settled among Europeans, Germany pursued the idea of *Lebensraum*,[62] which entailed the search for new lands to settle Germany's exploding population. *Lebensraum* was the term used by the leading German scientist and geographer, Friedrich Ratzel in his book, *Anthropogeography,* to argue that the development of a people into a (more complex) society was primarily influenced by their geographic condition. Ratzel said a society, which successfully adapted to one geographic territory would naturally and logically expand its national boundaries into another territory. To resolve German overpopulation, Ratzel proposed that Germany required overseas colonies to which its surplus people ought to emigrate. It was in pursuit of Ratzel's ideas of *Lebensraum* that imperialist leaders in Berlin ordered the extermination of the Herero and Nama peoples of Namibia (then known as German South West Africa) to clear the way for German settlers in the early twentieth century.[63]

It was in Africa, therefore, that the Germans first applied their nefarious racial theories, which justified the triumph of Europeans over other races. Africa was a testing ground used to construct the foundations upon which the Germans would further their genocidal wars and served as an initial site of human experimentation. *Lebensraum,* or the living space theory of Ratzel, was not only crucial in the German colonization of Africa but it also made available to German scientists the required human material for the further development of racial scientific studies that helped

---

[61] Adolf Hitler, *Mein Kampf* , Trans. Ralph Manheim (Boston: Houghton Mifflin, 1925).

[62] *Lebensraum* is the German word for "living space." It was developed as an ideology proposing German expansion. In 1901, the German ethnographer and geographer, Friedrich Ratzel coined the word Lebensraum ("living space"), as a term of human geography, to describe the importance of physical geography, or habitat as a factor that influences the human activities possible in the course of a people developing into a society.

[63] Friedrich Ratzel produced the foundations of human geography in his two-volume *Anthropogeographie* in 1882 and 1891. In 1897, he published his work on political geography, *Politische Geographie.* It was in these works that Ratzel introduced concepts that contributed to *Lebensraum* and *Social Darwinism.* His three volume work, *The History of Mankind,* was published in English in 1896 and contained over one thousand engravings and remarkable chromolithography.

feed the ideological sources upon which national socialism originated in Germany and carried out the extermination of the Jewish population of Europe. In his book, *From Africa to Auschwitz: How German South West Africa Incubated Ideas and Methods Adopted and Developed by the Nazis in Eastern Europe,* historian Benjamin Madley examined how the German experience in Namibia, with the extermination of the Herero and Nama people, was a crucial precursor to Nazi colonialism and genocide in Europe during the 1940s.[64]

Madley argues that it was the personal connections (literature and public debates) from the colony that helped communicate colonialist and genocidal ideas and methods from the Namibian concentration camps to the killing fields of Auschwitz in Germany. A key figure in this experimental research and study was a notable German scientist named Eugene Fischer.

Fischer was among Europe's most prominent medical scientists during the first half of the twentieth century. A professor of medicine, anthropology, and eugenics (a racist science that aimed to improve the genetic features of human populations through selective breeding and sterilization). Fischer rose to prominence in Germany following studies he conducted on the skeletal remains of African prisoners of war in the concentrations camps in Namibia during the genocidal massacres of Herero communities by German colonial armies led by General Lotta von Trotta. Fischer's sterilization experiments in German South-West Africa (Namibia) in the early 1900s were largely done on mixed-race offspring of the German army in order to provide justification to outlaw mixed-race marriages.[65] The literature that emerged out of Fischer's study on the human remains of African victims of the Namibian genocide and his sterilization experiments on mixed-race children of German soldiers became instrumental in German eugenic studies. He was appointed rector of the Frederick William University of Berlin by Adolf Hitler in 1933 and became director of the Kaiser Wilhelm Institute of Anthropology, Human Heredity, and Eugenics between 1927 and 1942. The Institute received skulls and other remains of African victims from the German concentration camps in Namibia, sold to German doctors, universities, and museums by colonial troops for medical experimentation and study by Fischer.[66]

Through the Kaiser Wilhelm Institute, supported by the Rockefeller Foundation in the United States, Fischer advanced his studies on eugenics. Through Fischer's work, the Eugenic Movement of race scientists in the United States established direct relationships with experimental studies and programs of

---

[64] Benjamin Madley, "From Africa to Auschwitz: How German South West Africa Incubated Ideas and Methods Adopted and Developed by the Nazis in Eastern Europe," *European History Quarterly* 35, no. 3: (2005): pp. 429-464.

[65] David Olusoga, and Erichsen, Casper W, *The Kaiser's Holocaust. Germany's Forgotten Genocide and the Colonial Roots of Nazism* (London: Faber and Faber, 2010).

[66] See, for example, Clarence Lusane, *Hitler's black victims: The historical experiences of Afro-Germans, European Blacks, Africans, and African Americans in the Nazi era* (London and New York: Routledge, 2002) pp. 12-13.

the Kaiser Wilhelm Institute in Germany. The Kaiser Wilhelm Institute regularly received human body parts, including eyes and skulls to be analyzed by Dr. Josef Mengele at Auschwitz in continuation of Fischer's eugenic studies, to prove Nazi racial theories and justify race-related social policies. There is now abundant material evidence linking Nazi race policies and those of eugenicists in the United States.[67]

The racial scientific theories developed from Morton to Cartwright and Darwin to Ratzel became instrumental in defining the political and economic history of the world in the early to mid-twentieth century. Slavery, colonialism, and the global economic exploitation of the world by Europeans would not have been possible without the fundamental collaborative role assumed by western scientists within this historical process. The evolutionary history of western experimental science can, therefore, not be separated from the general history of global destruction created by the politico-military forces of Europe (supported by ravenous economic giants) in Africa and elsewhere. It was the symbiotic relationship between experimental science and politics that simultaneously created the resources, both material and human, which transformed the economic conditions of Euro-Americans and eventually resulted in the further development of knowledge responsible for today's advancements in western education, agriculture, architecture, engineering, and medicine. Germany, which was at the forefront of capitalist industrialization in Europe at the time, had some of the leading western scientists of the era and led in defining the field of experimental medicine and eventually epidemiological studies.

Victims of Western Medical Research and Experimentation

The German medical experiments carried out by Fischer on the human remains of African victims of the German genocide in the concentration camps in Namibia was only the beginning of European medical research in Africa. The tradition of transforming African countries into vast laboratories for western clinical trials by large scale pharmaceutical companies, medical research institutions, and universities, have continued today with the transition to neocolonial rule. All across contemporary Africa, stories relating to unethical medical experimentation, clinical trials, the application of human subject studies lacking properly informed consent, and even forced medical procedures persist in nearly all major parts of the continent. The contemporary histories of epidemiological outbreaks in Africa and the accompanying western medical interventions have not been free from such practices: the deliberate use of disease outbreaks by western medical corporations and academic institutions to experiment vaccines and unapproved drug treatments without consent and knowledge of the subjects is a reality on the

---

[67] Edwin Black, "Eugenics and the Nazis - The California Connection," *SFGate.com, San Francisco Chronicle.* 9 November 2003, Web. 20 November 2013.

continent.

Many African communities have become victims of intentionally administered deadly medical research and experimentation. In March 2000, for example, Werner Bezwoda, a cancer researcher at South Africa's Witwatersrand University, was dismissed following reports of medical experiments involving very high doses of chemotherapy that he conducted on black breast-cancer patients allegedly without their knowledge or consent.[68] There was also the case of Richard McGowan, a Scottish anesthesiologist working in Zimbabwe, who was accused of five murders and convicted for the deaths of two infant patients in 2005. He had injected the infants with lethal doses of morphine. Another medical doctor, Michael Swango, was convicted of murder after pleading guilty to killing three American patients with lethal injections of potassium. He was also held on allegations of causing the deaths of sixty Zimbabweans and Zambians during the 1980s and 1990s.

The history of colonialism in Southern Africa is particularly replete with stories of how colonialists' officials, with the aid of medical doctors, used lethal medical practices as part of the state's response strategy to resistance and dissent. South Africa's apartheid regime, in particular, was very notorious in its use of biochemical methods to contain anti-colonialist efforts. During South Africa's Truth and Reconciliation Commission (TRC) proceedings, colonial army officials who worked with Wouter Basson, head of the apartheid regime's Project Coast (South Africa's Chemical and Biological Weapons Unit at the time) made shocking revelations of how they carried out the systematic killings of African freedom fighters in South Africa and Namibia with injected poisons from 1979 to 1987.[69] There is also the gruesome details of the apartheid regime's program of "forced sexual reassignment," a project carried out in South Africa from the 1970s to 1980s by Dr. Aubrey Levin, who forced white lesbian and gay soldiers to undergo "sex-change operations" designed to purge homosexuality within the apartheid army. The procedure, involving chemical castration, electric shock, and other unethical medical experiments, were carried out on an estimated nine hundred individuals, many of whom were between the ages of sixteen to twenty-four years old, both male and female. In the 1970s also, the colonial government of Zimbabwe (formerly Rhodesia) approved the deliberate and forceful use of Depo-Provera, a hormonal birth-control drug, on African women working in white-run commercial

---

[68] Shannon Brownlee, Winters, Dan, "Bad Science and Breast Cancer". *Discover Magazine*, 1 August 2002, Web. 24 Dec. 2012.

[69] Gould, Chandré (2006) *"South Africa's Chemical and Biological Warfare Programme 1981–1995"*, PhD thesis. Rhodes University. "Project Coast" was a top-secret chemical and biological weapons (CBW) program instituted by the South African apartheid regime against African freedom fighters during the apartheid era. It was a CBW program, which mainly produced the lethal agents CX powder and mustard gas; as well as non-lethal tear gas for anti-apartheid riot control purposes. Wouter Basson, a cardiologist and then personal physician of the South African Prime Minister, PW Botha, directed "Project Coast". Also see, for additional example, Helen E. Purkitt, Stephen F. Burgess: *"South Africa's Weapons of Mass Destruction"*. Indiana University Press, Bloomington 2005.

farms as part of a state sponsored population control program.[70]

Most African communities that have witnessed epidemiological outbreaks have reported very chilling stories of their experiences with western medical research. In 1994 in Zimbabwe, for example, the United States was implicated in an HIV/AIDS drug trials using AZT in a project jointly funded by the United States Centers for Disease Control (CDC) and World Health Organization (WHO). The collaborative research, conducted on HIV-positive Africans by American physicians and the University of Zimbabwe, were done without proper consent and included over seventeen thousand women who received trial medication that supposedly prevented mother-to-child transmission of HIV/AIDS. The subjects did not fully understand the testing methods, the effectiveness, the possible dangers, or the nature of a placebo in testing situations.[71] Reports indicate that many of them were coerced into participation in the clinical trials. These controversial experiments also resulted in the deaths of an approximated one thousand babies who contracted HIV/AIDS as a result of the trials.

Scandalous events such as these continue to implicate leading western physicians and multinational corporations in ongoing unethical medical research and clinical trials in Africa. These unethical practices often take place under the watchful eyes of the African scientific community and with willing collaboration of the African ruling elite. The extent of large-scale multinational corporate exploitation of Africa's resources cannot be divorced from these medical travesties. In many instances, epidemiological outbreaks in Africa have been triggered by the economic forces driving scientific research, such as corporate conquests and experimentation. On other occasions, leading pharmaceutical companies and other medical entities have regarded epidemiological catastrophes as convenient opportunities for medical experimentation and clinical trials. Perhaps the most disturbing revelation exemplifying such a scenario was the scandal that followed the West African meningitis outbreak of the 1990s in northern Nigeria, when the leading United States pharmaceutical company, Pfizer was accused of clinical trials involving the uncertified use of a new antibiotic called Trovan.

The clinical trial, conducted by Pfizer in 1996 in Kano, Nigeria, was done during the meningococcal meningitis outbreak in West Africa, the worst known meningitis outbreak in Sub-Saharan Africa. To test its new antibiotic trovafloxacin, known as Trovan, Pfizer gave one hundred children trovafloxacin while another hundred received the gold-standard anti-meningitis treatment ceftriaxone, a cephalosporin antibiotic.

---

[70] See, for example, Kaler, Amy. 1998. *"A Threat to the Nation and a Threat to the Men: the Banning of Depo-Provera in Zimbabwe, 1981".* Journal of Southern African Studies 24(2):p 347. Also see: Washington, Harriet A. *"Medical Apartheid"*, Anchor Books 2006 p394.

[71] Meier, Benjamin Mason: *"International Protection of Persons Undergoing Medical Experimentation: Protecting the Right of Informed Consent"*, Berkeley Journal of International Law (1085-5718) Meier yr:2002 vol:20 iss:3 pg:513 -554.

Pfizer gave the children a substantially reduced dose of the ceftriaxone relative to that approved by the United States Food and Drug Agency. Pfizer is said to have done this to skew the test in favor of its own drug. Five children given trovafloxacin died, as did six of those given ceftriaxone. The Nigerian government called the clinical trial "an illegal use of an unregistered drug." It alleged that participants and their families were not told that they were part of a trial nor that Médecins Sans Frontières (MSF) was offering the standard treatment in another part of the same building. Pfizer later acknowledged to reducing the dose of the standard treatment but said this was done to minimize injection-site pain, and that the mortality rates in both the trovafloxin and ceftriaxone arms of its trial were lower than among those treated with chloramphenicol by MSF.[72]

The survivors of the trial later pursued legal action against Pfizer in the United States, which subsequently led to an out of court US$75 million settlement that was subject to a confidentiality clause. Overall, the 1996-meningitis epidemic in northern Nigeria killed about twelve thousand people.[73] These deaths were principally associated with the human subject research deliberately carried out by Pfizer on patients who had come to treatment centers with the hope of receiving genuine health care. The possibility is that those deaths would have been averted or minimized had Pfizer not exploited the outbreak as an opportunity to experiment its newly developed antibiotic, Trovan, on the patients. Pfizer's responsibility for the deaths was associated with its choice to use its own drug (Trovan), which had never been used to treat meningitis, as opposed to chloramphenicol, the clinically approved drug that was being used in the outbreak by MSF and other responders.

This Trovan scandal has had severe implications and consequences for western epidemiological intervention and disease control in West Africa in recent years. In Nigeria, the Trovan controversy left a legacy of deep-rooted distrust for western medicine. Writing about this situation in an editorial in the *New York Times* on July 31, 2007, Harriet Washington observed that such events spread a fear of medicine throughout Africa, even in countries where Western doctors have not practiced in significant numbers.[74] "It is a fear the continent can ill afford when medical care is already hard to come by," Washington noted, adding that the distrust of Western medical workers had direct consequences in places like Nigeria, Chad, and Burkina Fasso, where since 2003 polio has been on the rise due to avoidance of vaccinations based upon the belief that they are contaminated with HIV or disguised sterilization agents.

During the 2014 Ebola outbreak, stories of community resistance against

---

[72] Senan Murray, "Africa: Anger at Deadly Nigerian drug trials," *BBC News Online*, 20 June 2007, Web. 11 July, 2015.

[73] "Nigerians Sue Pfizer Over Test Deaths," *BBC News Online,* 30 August 2001, Web. 22 May 2015.

[74] Harriet A. Washington, *"Why Africa Fears Western Medicine."* *The New York Times* (New York, NY) July 31, 2007.

foreign health workers and aid agencies were rampant in all three affected countries: Guinea, Liberia, and Sierra Leone.

On September 19, 2014, for example, international media went wild after reports emerged that eight Ebola aid workers and journalists had been murdered and dumped in a latrine in a remote village near the city of Nzerekore in Guinea by angry villagers.[75] Media reports stated that the delegation had arrived in the village to carry out disinfection work and educate people about Ebola prevention measures when angry residents attacked them with rocks and machetes, accusing the health workers of spreading the disease.

Similar protests had occurred in Sierra Leone two months earlier on July 26, 2014, when thousands marched on an Ebola treatment center in Kenema, eastern Sierra Leone, after a former nurse alleged that the deadly virus was invented to conceal "cannibalistic rituals" at the treatment ward in the area. The nurse told a market audience that the Kenema Government Hospital was engaged in a project of harvesting human organs and blood that was being sold to foreign pharmaceutical corporations. Following this public allegation, angry crowds immediately gathered outside the country's main Ebola hospital, where dozens of infected persons were reportedly receiving treatment for the virus, and threatened to burn it down. Police intervened and fired tear gas to disperse the crowds, and a nine-year-old boy was shot in the leg by a police officer's bullet.[76] A few days before this incident, family members of another woman alleged to have tested positive of the virus, stormed a clinic in Freetown and forcefully removed her from the hospital on suspicion that doctors were trying to kill her with an injection. In early August 2014, residents of the West Point community of Monrovia in Liberia also attacked a quarantine center and looted mattresses while helping suspected Ebola patients to leave the facility.[77] The attack followed reports that the treatment facility was spreading the virus in the community. Armed troops intervened to put down the protests and shot a teenager in the process.

The allegations and rumors these Africans heaped on the foreign health workers are not farfetched. They are well-founded fears and suspicions that continuously surround western medical interventions in epidemiological outbreaks in Africa. Their rationality is solidly etched on the history of western medical research and experimentation on the continent from the days of slavery to colonialism and the present era.

---

[75] Abby Philip, "Eight dead in attack on Ebola team in Guinea. Killed in cold blood." *Washington Post* (Washington DC) September 18, 2014. Also see, 'Eight reported dead in attack on Ebola workers in Guinea" by Robyn Dixon. *Los Angeles Times* (Los Angeles, CA) September 18, 2014 (www.latimes.com/world/africa/la-fg-attack-ebola-guinea-outreach-20140918-story.html).

[76] See also, "Protesters March on Ebola Center in Sierra Leone," *Newsweek* (New York, NY) July 26, 2014, (www.newsweek.com/protesters-march-ebola-center-sierra-leone-261467) Web. 15 July 2015.

[77] "Ebola Crisis: Confusion as Patients Vanish in Liberia," *BBC Online* (London, United Kingdom) August 17, 2014, (www.bbc.com/news/world-africa-28827091) Web. 5 2015.

In late December 2014, for instance, a report emerged of a controversy relating to a team of British doctors attached to an Ebola treatment center in Freetown who accused an Italian NGO of using an untested drug on patients who had reportedly tested positive for the Ebola virus.[78]

The team of fourteen British doctors, nurses, and paramedics ceased operations at the Lakka Treatment Center in Freetown on allegations that the Italian NGO Emergency was involved in the experimental use of an untested drug called Amiodarone on several Ebola patients. The British medical team reported that its members couldn't work in the environment because the complications involved in administering the drug to the patients put health workers at grave risk. They alleged that two doctors, one of whom was a Ugandan, were infected at the center, and that Amiodarone was, in fact, administered at the center without patient consent and was responsible for the mortality figures at the center. Amiodarone is a licensed drug to regulate patients' heartbeat and was not approved for clinical trials on Ebola patients when the Italian NGO reportedly used it at the center. At the time of this report, the Italian NGO operated in a twenty two-bed facility at Lakka and another one hundred-bed facility at Goderich in Freetown, funded by the British Department for International Development (DFID). The British doctors who protested against the experimental trial at the facility complained of the matter to DFID, but there were no reports of any punitive measures taken against the NGO. The families of those who allegedly died as a consequence of the trial were not told of the incident. This scandalous story later appeared in the *Guardian* newspaper in London on December 22, 2014, but neither the government of Sierra Leone nor any of the agencies involved in the Ebola epidemiological response, including DFID that was funding the operation of the Emergency, issued any public statement in response to the facts of the matter. There has never been a disclosure on the total number of patients who reportedly died as a consequence of Amiodarone.[79]

The Amiodarone incident was not a uniquely isolated event and was probably part of a successive chain of experimental cases that occurred in West Africa with the Ebola outbreak. Several communities and individual households with surviving Ebola victims, have recounted harrowing stories of their experiences at Ebola treatment facilities in the region. These astounding stories, sometimes too horrifying to sound true, can be heard all over West Africa in almost all communities affected by the epidemic. They relate to severe allegations of medical research and experimentation, similar to what was done on patients without their knowledge or

---

[78] Robtel Pailey, "Treating Africans with an Untested Ebola Drug", *Aljazeera*, January 3, 2015 (www.aljazeera.com/indepth/opinion/2014/12/treating-africans-with-anunte2014123195838317148.html). 20 June 2015.

[79] Sarah Bosley, "Untested Ebola Drug Given to Patients in Sierra Leone Causes UK Walkout" *The Guardian*, December 22, 2014 (www.theguardian.com/world/2014/dec/22/ebola-untested-drug-patients-sierra-leone-uk-staff-leave) Web. 20 June 2015.

consent by groups like Emergency in the treatment centers of Freetown.

While international organizations and local authorities blamed the explosive nature of the virus on the cultural behaviors of West African communities – the practice of caring for the sick and washing of the dead – there also exists overwhelming counter accusations from local communities against national and international actors of deliberately spreading Ebola in the region to create tools of biochemical warfare for western nations and profit for the global pharmaceutical industry. These accusations, overwhelming as they are, have been dismissed as conspiracy theory and disregarded in the wider western media coverage and academic discourse on the epidemic.

Western media coverage of anti-Ebola resistance efforts hinged on the usual fabricated accusations of community people's denial of the existence of the virus. Western journalists deliberately ignored or chose to suppress the actual causes of the dissent created both by the "mysterious nature" of the epidemic and the repressive character of the national and international response mechanism. They did not examine why in Sierra Leone, for example, the government's authoritarian policy of brutal lockdowns and repressive quarantine measures failed to mitigate the rising numbers of infections and deaths. By December 2014, Sierra Leone had the highest number of daily infections and deaths according to official statistics. It must at least be considered that the repressive government measures were potentially part of a population containment strategy aimed at suppressing dissent and resistance to state authority because of the lack of real state commitments to ending the virus.

Isolated protests by health workers and community residents against Ebola aid workers and national containment efforts were not simply the result of denial of the existence of the virus. Instead, the dissent of Africans was actually a reasonable response to authoritarian national disease policies and the prevalent reports and testimonies from victims' families about clinical wrong-doings in treatment centers.

Some of this information, which initially existed as rumors, materialized into actual news stories, but leading newspapers in Europe largely ignored them. A case in point was an incident on February 26, 2015, when personnel of the Sierra Leone Office of National Security (ONS) intercepted a consignment of 2,592 blood samples contained in 72 boxes and 36 vials at the Lungi International Airport in Sierra Leone. The blood samples were confirmed to be from people infected with the Ebola virus and were reportedly obtained at the National Institute for Communicable Diseases at Lakka in Freetown. Sierra Leone's Health Ministry said in a statement following the scandal that the highly infectious blood samples were meant for safe storage in South Africa, which it claimed had the only maximum containment laboratory in Africa.[80] But documentary evidence

---

[80] Kemoh Cham, "Fears over intercepted Ebola Blood Samples," *Africa Reviews*, February 28, 2015.(Web: www.africareview.com/News/Fears-over-intercepted-Ebola-blood-samples/-/979180/2638476/-/k3w0gj/-/index.

that accompanied the intercepted shipment indicated that the blood shipment, weighing 250 kilos, was actually destined for Belgium on a Brussels Airline flight, leaving the evening of that day. Independent testimonies from leading airport workers revealed that the intercepted blood consignment was actually the sixth shipment in a successive process that was ongoing since the Ebola outbreak. The embarrassing scandal caused a presidential dismissal of the head of the national security agency whose personnel had actually intercepted the said consignment and brought it to the public domain. No other individual from the health ministry was arrested or dismissed. This major story was never reported by any of the western journalists who were stationed in the region covering the Ebola epidemic.[81]

These suspicious events fed into the numerous allegations from ordinary people across the region that questioned the actual origins of the virus and its real modes of transmission. Competing stories around the origin of the 2014 Ebola virus in West Africa are many among local communities in the region, and dismissing these accounts with a simple wave of the hand will do little to convince the community victims of this catastrophic medical tragedy and the many ghosts it has created, to forget the devastation they have endured.

---

html),

[81] "President Koroma, "There can be no development without security," Press Release of the State House Communication Unit, 5 Aug. 2015 (www.statehouse.gov.sl/index.php/useful-links/1257-qthere-can-be-no-development-without-securityq-president-koroma).

CHAPTER 3

ORIGIN OF WEST AFRICA'S EBOLA OUTBREAK: AN ALTERNATIVE NARRATIVE

Things here have been very hectic and I will have to keep this short, but I wanted to inform you that Dr. (Aniru) Conteh recently received an accidental needle stick while caring for a pregnant woman with Lassa. As you know, the ward is understaffed and he had been drawing the blood himself. Despite treatment and our best efforts, Dr. Conteh became severely ill. I am afraid to report that he died of Lassa fever over the weekend. I think he actually made it through the acute disease, but passed away from renal failure...
– Ross I. Donaldson, The Lassa Ward.[82]

The death of Sierra Leone's leading viral hemorrhagic fever specialist, Dr. Sheikh Umar Khan, during the first few weeks of the 2014 Ebola outbreak, generated world news headlines. Khan died on July 29, 2014, in the eastern district of Kailahun in Sierra Leone. Khan was reportedly infected on July 22 at the Kenema Government Hospital where he presided over the treatment of Lassa fever at a sixteen-bed unit on the ground floor of the hospital. The thirty-nine year-old father of two spent ten years as a physician and was the leading virologist in the country at the time of his death. When asked a month before his death about the risks faced by health workers in Sierra Leone fighting against an emerging Ebola epidemic, Khan told *BBC's* Freetown correspondent, Umaru Fofana, "I'm afraid for my life. I must say I cherish my life, and if you are afraid of it you will take the maximum precautions."[83]

---

[82] Ross I. Donaldson, "The Lassa Ward: One Man's Fight Against One of the World's Deadliest Diseases," *St. Martin's Press,* 2009.

[83] Umaru Fofana, "Leading Ebola Doctor Sheik Umar Khan Dies," *BBC News,* July 30, 2014 (www.bbc.com/news/world-africa-28560507).

Khan's death raised a serious question across western medical circles: why did the western doctors working with him refuse to treat him with a known, potentially effective experimental drug? The said experimental drug is called *ZMapp* and was being tested at a field laboratory in Kailahun. A group of scientists from Mapp Biopharmaceuticals, a biotech company in San Diego, the National Institute of Allergy and Infectious Diseases division of the National Institute of Health, and the Public Health Agency of Canada's research facility in Winnipeg developed *ZMapp* a decade earlier. A single dose of *ZMapp* was within reach of that remote field hospital in rural Sierra Leone where Khan was reportedly admitted after he tested positive for Ebola.

In June of 2014, a few weeks before Khan fell ill, Gary Kobinger, one of the scientists responsible for the development of the experimental drug, and his group in Canada travelled to Sierra Leone with laboratory equipment for the doctors working at the newly established Ebola treatment center in Kailahun run by MSF. Kobinger left three plastic bottles of *ZMapp* in a freezer at the Kailahun treatment center. He wanted to see how *ZMapp* held up in the tropical climate, where the heat and an uncertain electricity supply can ruin the drug's effectiveness.[84]

When Khan became ill, a government official in Freetown reportedly sent an e-mail correspondence to Ebola experts around the world seeking assistance on how to treat the country's only hemorrhagic fever specialist.[85] The cry for help is claimed to have resulted in a chain of international conference calls involving scientists and health officials from various parts of the world who represented the WHO, the United States Centers for Disease Control and Prevention, the Public Health Agency of Canada, the United States Army, MSF, and the government of Sierra Leone. The debate centered on the single dose of *ZMapp* that had been left by Kobinger at the Kailahun Ebola treatment center a month earlier.

Western doctors profess to have debated endlessly and could not reach a decision whether to administer the drug to Sierra Leone's leading virologist. They argued that the drug had never been tested on humans, and they allegedly feared the potential consequences that could result should an allergic reaction from it kill Dr. Khan. They said his blood showed antibodies to the virus, evidence that his own immune system was already in full battle against the Ebola virus.

"What if the drug got in the way of that immune response?" they asked. Nearly all those involved in the discussion knew Dr. Sheikh Umarr Khan and they knew the question was a matter of life and death. A unanimous decision was never reached and Khan eventually died on July 29, 2014. Reports indicate that

---

[84] Richard Preston's "Inside the Ebola Wars," *The New Yorker*, October 27, 2014 (www.newyorker.com/magazine/2014/10/27/ebola-wars).

[85] Kelly Crowne, 'Dying Sierra Leone Dr. Sheik Umar Khan Never Told Ebola Drug was Available," *CBC News*, August 18, 2014 (www.cbc.ca/news/health/dying-sierra-leone-dr-sheik-umar-khan-never-told-ebola-drug-was-available-1.2738163).

Khan's input or consent was never sought. His family reports that they were also never consulted about the debate that decided his fate. In Sierra Leone, news of Khan's death was a national shock. A state of panic instantly gripped the entire country and it marked the transition towards a grim reality: Ebola was now a real possibility in people's' lives. The following morning, the government declared a state of public health emergency with a string of measures involving travel restrictions and bans on public gatherings.

Ernest Bai Koroma, president of Sierra Leone, addressed the grieving nation in a televised statement following Khan's death. Koroma said, "Extraordinary challenges require extraordinary measures. The Ebola virus disease poses an extraordinary challenge to our nation...I hereby proclaim a state of public emergency to enable us to take a more robust approach to deal with the Ebola outbreak." He also cancelled a trip to a summit of around fifty African leaders in Washington DC that was scheduled the following week. Koroma's statement came a day after his counterpart in Liberia, Ellen Johnson Shirleaf, adopted similar measures.

But Liberia, faced with the same exploding epidemic, had attracted huge international media coverage relating to another devastating news story: a fifty-nine-year-old American health worker named Nancy Writebol and a thirty-three year old American doctor named Kent Brantly, both working with the United States Christian charity Samaritan's Purse at the ELWA hospital in Monrovia, tested positive for Ebola. This was around the same time that Sheikh Umar Khan was on the verge of death in the MSF-run Ebola treatment center in the eastern district of Kailahun, while international officials from Washington to Winnipeg and Geneva were failing to reach a consensus on a treatment of *ZMapp* that would have potentially saved his life.

Unlike Khan, whose fate was decided without his input, Writebol and Brantly were given the opportunity to make choices. When their results were confirmed positive, CDC officials in Atlanta, the United States Embassy in Monrovia, and doctors of Samaritan's Purse consulted with Brantly and Writebol regarding a decision to use experimental drugs to treat them. Several experimental drugs and vaccines were discussed with the Ebola patients including *ZMapp*. Following the discussion, and based on the patients' choice, *ZMapp* was eventually selected.[86] On July 28, 2014, (a day before Khan's death in Kailahun), CDC officials and the United States Embassy in Monrovia contacted Gary Kobinger, the scientist at the Public Health Agency of Canada who left the single dose of *ZMapp* at the Kailahun Ebola treatment center, about the situation of the two American Ebola aid workers. Kobinger told the officials that the drug was sitting in a laboratory freezer in Kailahun, in Sierra Leone, across the international border. It had to be flown quickly from Kailahun to Monrovia if it was to save the two American

---

[86] See, for example, "Inside the Ebola Wars" in *The New Yorker*, October 27, 2014.

patients. The United States Embassy in Monrovia sent Lisa Hensley, a CDC official stationed in Monrovia and a colonel in the United States Marine Corps, in a chartered Russian Mi-8 helicopter flown by two Ukrainian pilots to pick up the drug from Kailahun. Khan died the same day the drug that held his only chance for survival was taken away to Monrovia to treat the two American aid workers suffering from the same Ebola infection. In Monrovia, the three bottles of *ZMapp* from Kailahun ended up saving the lives of Brantly and Writebol before they were evacuated to the Emory University Hospital in Atlanta. Both patients were at the final stages of life when they received a single bottle of the experimental drug and were evacuated to the United States.[87]

"I am thrilled to be alive, to be well and to be reunited with my family. Through the care of the Samaritan's Purse and SIM missionary team in Liberia, the use of an experimental drug, and the expertise and resources of the health care team at Emory University Hospital, God saved my life; a direct answer to thousands and thousands of prayers," Kent Brantly told a news conference following his discharge at the Emory University Hospital in Atlanta.[88] But the prayers and the God that saved Kent Brantly and Nancy Writebol from death were absent and could not save the life of Sheikh Umar Khan, Sierra Leone's only virologist, who had faced the Ebola epidemic singlehandedly in Kenema.

The government of Sierra Leone called Khan a national hero after his death. His colleagues in Freetown and around the world spoke glowingly about his character and dedication to medical service. But unlike Brantly and Writebol, Sheikh Umar Khan can never recount his experiences fighting against Ebola nor tell anyone how he actually contracted the virus.

The reason as to why *Zmapp* was offered to the American aid workers but not to Dr. Khan has produced competing stories within Sierra Leone and across West Africa, and like many other controversial issues that accompanied the Ebola outbreak, it is still part of the many questions that have been left unsatisfactorily addressed. At the heart of these conflicting stories and unanswered questions lie the contradictory history of international humanitarianism and the questionable goals of western interventionist activity in conflict resolution, crisis prevention, and disaster management efforts in Africa. In the case of the 2014 health catastrophe in West Africa, the sordid history of Western aid in times of catastrophe becomes central to understanding the alternative narrative on the actual origin of the 2014 Ebola epidemic and its modes of transmission in West Africa.

---

[87] See *The New Yorker* October 27, 2014 Issue for additional details.

[88] From transcript of statement by Kent Brantly given at news conference held Aug. 21, 2014, the day he was discharged from Emory University Hospital, Atlanta, GA. (news.emory.edu/stories/2014/08/ebola_press_conference_brantly_statement/campus.html). Brantley later published a memoir titled, *Called for Life*, in which he documented his experience with Ebola and eventual treatment at Emory University Hospital.

Lassa Fever: A Basis for Understanding the 2014 Outbreak

Khan's death bitterly conveyed into the homes of Sierra Leoneans the vicious death message of the Ebola epidemic, and along with it, awakened in the country the ghostly memory of Khan's predecessor, Dr. Aniru Conteh, who died ten years earlier in 2004 at the Kenema Government Hospital's Lassa Fever Ward. Conteh died after he was accidentally infected by a needle stick while drawing blood from a pregnant woman who had tested positive for Lassa fever.

Lassa fever was first identified in the town of Lassa, in the Borno State of Nigeria in 1969 after two missionary nurses in the Nigerian town of Lassa died of a dramatic fever and a third nurse named Penny Pinneo was diagnosed with similar symptoms before being evacuated to the United States on a routine Pan Am flight from Lagos.[89] When Pinneo arrived in the United States, Dr. John Frame of Columbia University collected blood samples from the patient and sent it to the Yale Arbovirus Research Unit. No biosafety procedures were adopted during the initial investigation into the unknown disease. This resulted into two fatal laboratory based infections in the United States: a laboratory technician at the Yale Arbovirus Research Unit died and a senior researcher contracted the mysterious fever but survived. Following this incident at the Yale Laboratory, investigation into the virus was moved to a CDC containment laboratory in Atlanta. The disease was then named Lassa fever, a deadly viral hemorrhagic fever that combines persistent fever, muscular pain, nausea, diarrhea, and red eyes (similar symptoms to Ebola) and which can infect humans with devastating outcomes.[90]

While the CDC continued its study of the Lassa virus in its containment facilities in Atlanta, in West Africa Lassa fever continued to claim more casualties throughout the late 1960s and early 1970s.

In 1972 several outbreaks of Lassa fever in the towns of Tongo and Panguma in eastern Sierra Leone marked the genesis of the viral hemorrhagic fever in the Mano River region of West Africa. After the 1972 outbreaks in Sierra Leone, the CDC, which was still investigating the virus in its containment facilities in Atlanta, established research stations in Segbwema, Kenema, and Panguma (all in the eastern parts of the country) to carryout field studies on the virus. A treatment program was set-up in Segbwema at the Nixon Memorial Mission Hospital[91] and Dr. Aniru Conteh, a viral hemorrhagic fever specialist, was recruited in 1979 to serve as the CDC team leader in Sierra Leone in the ongoing effort to study

---

[89] Frame JD, Baldwin JM, Gocke DJ, Troup JM (1 July 1970). "Lassa fever, a new virus disease of man from West Africa. I. Clinical description and pathological findings," *Am. J. Trop. Med. Hyg.* 19, no. 4): 670–6 (1 July 1970).

[90] Richmond, J. K.; Baglole, D. J., "Lassa fever: Epidemiology, Clinical Features, and Social Consequences". *BMJ* 327, no. 7426 (2003): pp. 1271–1275.

[91] Keane, E; Gilles, HM, "Lassa fever in Panguma Hospital, Sierra Leone, 1973-6". *British Medical Journal* 1, no. 6073 (1977): pp. 1399–402.

the Lassa virus. Dr. Conteh earned his bachelor's degree from Durham University and graduated from the medical school of the University of Ibadan in Nigeria. He was working at Ibadan Teaching Hospital in Nigeria before his recruitment by the CDC in 1979 for its Lassa research program in Sierra Leone.[92]

With the outbreak of the civil war in 1991, the CDC abandoned the Lassa fever research program and pulled out of Sierra Leone in 1993, leaving Dr. Conteh behind. He would later relocate the Lassa treatment program to the Kenema Government Hospital. After the departure of the CDC from Sierra Leone, the Lassa ward was left largely without support. The ward continued to function due solely to the guidance and commitment of Dr. Conteh.

In 1996 there was a sporadic rise in Lassa cases in eastern Sierra Leone and Dr. Conteh, who was fighting the epidemic alone, appealed to the British medical relief organization, Merlin, who provided health promotion and treatment activities. Merlin later offered assistance aimed at developing the capacity of the Sierra Leone Ministry of Health and Sanitation to deal with Lassa. Merlin also raised funds for the construction of a laboratory, but this was not completed.[93]

From 1979 to 2004, Dr. Conteh treated thousands of patients with Lassa fever, building a monumental recognition as the world's leading expert on the management of the disease. He contributed significantly to the research on the disease. He spent over twenty-five years dealing with Lassa fever until March 2004, when he admitted a young, pregnant woman at the Lassa Ward of the Kenema Government Hospital. The patient was a volunteer nurse with the hospital's pediatric service. On March 17, 2004, after numerous unsuccessful attempts by staff members to obtain blood from the patient's arm, Dr. Conteh is said to have attempted femoral venipuncture and sustained a needle-stick injury in the process. The patient died the next day.[94] Dr. Conteh developed a fever a few days later, then profuse vomiting and diarrhea, followed by bleeding and renal failure and cardiac arrest. Medical experts around the world were consulted. On April 4, 2004, in the most absurd of ironies, Aniru Conteh, who had become a patient at the very ward he was instrumental in establishing and maintaining, died of the Lassa virus that he spent his entire life as a physician to combat.

But unlike his successor, Sheikh Umar Khan, who was infected through similar circumstances and died within the same area ten years later, Aniru Conteh's death was never regarded as a national tragedy, nor did it attract global media attention. No government official reportedly attended his funeral, which took place in Daru, Kailahun district (a place that later became the epicenter of the

---

[92] Ogbu O, Ajuluchukwu E, Uneke CJ, "Lassa fever in West African sub-region: an overview". *Journal of vector borne diseases* 44, no. 1 (2007): pp. 1–11.

[93] Keane, E; Gilles, HM, "Lassa fever in Panguma Hospital, Sierra Leone, 1973-6," *British Medical Journal* 1, no. 6073 (1977): pp. 139–402.

[94] Mellor, N., "Aniru Conteh," *BMJ* 328, no. 7447 (2004): 1078.

Ebola epidemic in 2014 and where Khan himself was taken to die ten years later).

"Mourners observed the conspicuous absence of people in authority," Sulaiman Momodu, a journalist who attended the funeral of Dr. Conteh organized by family members and friends, said. "While HIV/AIDS takes years to sentence somebody to death, the Lassa Fever virus is ruthlessly doing so in just few weeks," Momodu wrote in an article titled, "Lassa Fever: Who Is Next to Die?" published in the *Concord Times* on May 16, 2004.

Although Dr. Aniru Conteh's death was never breaking news in the international press, the devastating event marked the beginning of a new program that changed both the status of the Lassa fever program in Kenema and also the focus of international medical interests in West Africa. Immediately after Dr. Conteh's death, the United States Agency for International Development (USAID) established a task force to deal with Lassa fever. The task force brought stakeholders from Sierra Leone, Guinea, Liberia, the WHO, the European Union, and other Non-Governmental Organizations (NGOs). The United States government provided funds to WHO to coordinate the establishment of a Lassa Fever Laboratory at the Kenema Government Hospital in Sierra Leone.[95]

To carry out this program, a Mano River Union Lassa Fever Network (MRU-LFN) was formed to help strengthen scientific cooperation, patient management, outbreak surveillance, and laboratory capacity. The WHO conducted a site evaluation of Kenema and discovered that the construction of the Lassa Laboratory started by Merlin had been left unfinished at the time of Dr. Conteh's death. Central to the WHO/USAID plan was the building of a world-class laboratory on the site that Merlin had identified years ago. The laboratory would serve as an "international medical research center" for western scientists. The proposed Kenema Lassa Laboratory would then be connected to other laboratories in Guinea and Liberia as part of the Mano River Union Lassa Fever Network's agenda. The plan would also include the building of a new Lassa Isolation Ward at the Kenema Government Hospital, which would be funded by the European Union.

These international interests in Lassa fever, however, were not the result of Dr. Aniru Conteh's death, nor were they driven by humanitarian considerations to mitigate the virus. Rather, they were part of international initiatives necessitated by changing developments in the international political environment that opened up the global health landscape to an increasingly challenging security threat: the dangers of bioterrorism in the twenty-first century.

---

[95] Khan, SH; Goba, A; Chu, M; Roth, C; Healing, T; Marx, A; Fair, J; Guttieri, MC et al., "New opportunities for field research on the pathogenesis and treatment of Lassa fever," *Antiviral Research* 78, no. 1 (2008): 103–15.

Lassa fever: US Bioweapons Project and the 2014 Outbreak

Although western scientists always regarded Lassa fever as part of the dangerously new emerging diseases in Africa, the Lassa virus became a strategic question in the policy agenda of the United States after the September 11, 2001 airplane attacks and the anthrax incident that same year. Following these developments in Washington DC and New York, the Lassa virus was re-assessed for its possible use as a bioterrorist agent and was categorized by the United States CDC and United States National Institutes of Allergy and Infectious Diseases (NIAID) as a *Category A* agent. *Category A* is the highest risk level of any pathogenic agent with potential for use in bioterrorism. A pathogen is classified as such only on account of its ability to spread easily and cause major public health impacts, including high mortality. Around the time the CDC was considering the potential of Lassa's *weaponization*, outbreaks of avian flu and SARS had already raised the anxiety of policy makers in Washington about pandemics. Due to this security hysteria coming from Washington, Lassa fever was included as a notifiable disease under the WHO's revised International Health Regulations (IHR) due to its epidemic prone nature and potential to cause economic and social disruption.[96]

This heightened concern and control that characterized Lassa fever was driven principally by this prevailing international phenomenon of *securitization*.[97] It is a situation that caused previously disregarded pathogens to be included as critical subjects of the international discourse on existential threats to western safety and security after the 9/11 attacks and anthrax incidents in the United States. This trend became increasingly common in the international geopolitical landscape, which was now feeling threatened by the adverse forces of globalization and new security concerns.

These international security anxieties regarded the health situation in the Mano River countries of Sierra Leone, Liberia, and Guinea as significant bioterrorist breeding grounds. The civil wars of the 1990s opened up the region to similar international policy concerns: the potential of terrorist investments in the wars for access to strategic resources. The western conceptualization of the "blood diamond theory" did not come as a response to the role of western multinational monopolies over West Africa's diamonds, but how these monopolies, facing the risks of challenges by "international terrorist networks," already trading arms to subaltern armies and rebel groups in exchange for diamonds in the region, could be protected. The Lassa fever concerns were predated by these earlier western efforts to prevent groups listed by the United States as terrorists from profiting from the spoils created by the decade old wars raging in West Africa.

---

[96] Melone, J., "The Latent Threat of Lassa Fever," *Johns Hopkins Bloomberg School of Public Health,* 2009.

[97] Okeke, I. N., "Divining Without Seeds: The Case for Strengthening Laboratory Medicine in Africa". *Cornell University Press,* 2011.

In West Africa, where social and economic systems suffered complete ruin due to decades of multinational exploitation and state corruption, the recalibration and reclassification of Lassa fever within the realms of bioterrorist concerns must have been viewed as welcome news to local health officials. The new trajectory offered potential opportunities for resource mobilization and international funding. On the international level, networks of actors moved to promote specific courses of action and mobilized policy narratives and convincing storylines based on these new framings. Lassa fever was now an attractive investment for the political and institutional power sectors of the west.

Public health concerns of the World Health Organization in West Africa after the civil wars also painted Lassa fever as a threat to post-conflict re-development in the region.[98] But the recalibration and reclassification of the Lassa virus as a *Category A* pathogen did not only make it a question of regional and international security concern, but it also created an assemblage of diverse biodefense interests which opened-up funding incentives and research possibilities for western scientists and biotech companies to work on what was before now a neglected tropical disease in the rain forests of West Africa. This CDC classification turned Lassa fever into a threat against United States national security interests. This eventually resulted in serious international actions: a significant amount of the billions of dollars that were raised and set aside by the United States government for biodefense efforts since the anthrax incident in 2001 was now channeled towards laboratory research efforts in West Africa located at the Kenema Government Hospital in eastern Sierra Leone. This research work was aimed at supposedly strengthening the United States medical capacity to deal with a bioterrorist attack or outbreak intentionally unleashed against its military or civilian population.[99]

It was because of this that the United States' National Institute of Health (NIH) funded Tulane University's grant proposal entitled "Diagnostics For Biodefense," a proposal that regarded Lassa fever as having a potential to be used as a biological weapon directed against civilian or military targets. Tulane's proposal stated that the classification of the Lassa virus as a *Category A* pathogen necessitated the development of an "effective, highly sensitive, and cost-effective medical diagnostics for public health laboratories and hospital-based clinical laboratories to diagnose individuals exposed to and/or infected with the virus." The CDC already classified Lassa fever as a Biosafety Level 4 and NIAID Biodefense *Category A* agent.[100]

This Tulane University proposal received a budget of US$10 million from the

---

[98] Mirza, I. A., Khan, M. A., Hakim, A., "Lassa Fever UN Peacekeepers' Nightmare in West Africa". *Pakistan Armed Forces Medical Journal* 1, (2005).

[99] "Kenema Government Hospital," *Viral Hemorrhagic Fever Consortium*, 2011, Web 6 July 2015.

[100] Okeke, Iruka N.; Wain, John, "Post-genomic challenges for collaborative research in infectious diseases," *Nature Reviews Microbiology* (Nov. 2008).

National Institute of Health and a further US$15 million five-year grant focusing on the study of the pathogenesis of Lassa.[101] The Tulane grant was the largest biodefense allocation that opened up the Lassa Laboratory of the Kenema Government Hospital for field research. The portfolio of biodefense related projects in Kenema also included those of Metabiota, which had at least three grants from the Defense Threat Reduction Agency (DTRA) and Cooperative 10 Biological Engagement Program (CBEP), both of which are United States Department of Defense (DOD) agencies. Metabiota's efforts were concentrated primarily on the pathogenesis of Lassa fever, with applications for treatments and vaccines.

By 2010, this United States funded biodefense research on Lassa fever reached a climax with the establishment of a centralized organization, the Viral Hemorrhagic Fever Consortium (VHFC), to coordinate the array of institutions trooping into eastern Sierra Leone to execute biodefense research related projects. The Viral Hemorrhagic Fever Consortium comprises researchers from Tulane University, Scripps Research Institute, Broad Institute, Harvard University, University of California at San Diego, University of Texas Medical Branch, Autoimmune Technologies LLC, Corgenix Medical Corporation, Kenema Government Hospital, and the Irrua Specialist Teaching Hospital in Nigeria. The amount of biodefense dollars that flowed into Sierra Leone from 2009-2012 instantly transformed the once dilapidated and abandoned Lassa Ward of the Kenema Government Hospital, located on its small site in eastern Sierra Leone, into a considerable recipient of a well-funded international research program. In February 2011, for example, the *Reuters News Agency* reported that the Lassa research project at the Kenema Government Hospital cost around US$40 million in biodefense funding.[102] Another *Reuters* article published on February 14, 2014 described the Kenema laboratory as an outpost of the United States government's "war on terror," funded by bio-defense dollars with the purpose of limiting vulnerability of western interests to biological agents. An American researcher, Matt Boisen told *Reuters,* "There has been a renewed emphasis on those tropical diseases that government health officials consider bio-threats. It would be naive not to think some terrorist group could use one of these things to create terror."[103]

---

[101] Geisbert TW, Jones S, Fritz EA et al., "Development of a New Vaccine for the Prevention of Lassa Fever". *PLOS Med.* 2, no. 6: e183 (2005).

[102] Akam, Simon, *"United States Anti-terror Outpost Tackles Rat-borne Virus,"* *Reuters,* February 14, 2011 (www.reuters.com/article/2011/02/14/us-bioterror-africa-idUSTRE71D49820110214).

[103] Interview with Matt Boison conducted by Simon Akam of the *Reuters News Agency* in February 2011.

Western Biodefense Research Implications in the Mano River Region

The driving force behind these research efforts were entirely anchored on the security concerns of the United States and its European allies. Their objective was to understand mechanisms related to the human immune response to Lassa virus infections with the goal of developing treatments and vaccines. Although the recalibration of Lassa fever as a threat to international security necessitated the flow of several millions of dollars in biodefense funding, western scientists also debated the implications of the CDC's *Category A* classification. Some expressed doubts as to whether Lassa would make an effective bio-weapon because, for such a thing to happen, contact with infected bodily fluids was needed to transfer the disease from one human host to another. These questions and uncertainties about Lassa created the need and basis for additional scientific studies into the Lassa virus. This scientific enquiry applied DNA sequencing or the science of genomics. This also became a task of the VHFC, taken over by scientists at the Broad Institute of Harvard University. The researchers aimed at discovering the viral and host genetic factors that influence susceptibility and resistance to infection and disease. Pardis Sabeti, a specialist in reading and analyzing the genomes of organisms, led the genomics research conducted at the Broad Institute of MIT and Harvard University, exploring the way viruses change over time as they adapt to their environments. Sabeti and her team obtained blood samples of people infected with Lassa fever and read the genomes of whatever they could find in the patients' blood.

At the Kenema Government Hospital, these efforts were coordinated in a ward with a twelve-bed facility headed by Dr. Sheikh Umar Khan. Khan and Sabeti established strong friendship ties years ahead of the 2014 outbreak, *The New Yorker* reported in October 2014. Between October 2006 and October 2008, Dr. Khan received blood samples from patients with suspected Lassa fever submitted to the Lassa Diagnostic Laboratory in Kenema. The samples were collected in Sierra Leone, Liberia, and Guinea from the annual five hundred to seven hundred patients admitted at the hospital that were processed as part of the ongoing research at the Lassa Fever Laboratory for other viruses of interest. These samples were also sent to the Broad Institute where Sabeti and her team conducted their genomic studies. Sabeti told *The New Yorker* that Khan was fascinated by genomics and was curious to find out how the sequencing was done at the Broad Institute. He had planned to visit Harvard to join Pardis Sabeti and her team a few months before he died in July 2014 as a victim of the outbreak.[104]

In a research paper submitted to the United States' CDC documenting the outcome of this research, Khan and others revealed that over twenty-five percent of the suspected Lassa patients they studied held evidence of infections similar

---

[104] "Inside the Ebola Wars," *The New Yorker,* October 27, 2014.

to Ebola and Dengue fever. This study contradicts other scientific speculations, especially that of Fabian Leendertz and his team, which rashly located the primary infections of the epidemic in Miliandou, south of Guinea with the death of an infant on December of 2013. The findings of Khan and his colleagues, recorded in that report, had identified (at least since 2008) the evolutionary trend and mutational characteristics of the "virus" which developed in 2014 into a regional disaster and international health crisis. This fact was further amplified in a report published on August 28, 2014, by the journal, *Science*, detailing the results of a major surveillance study on "Ebola virus genomes" that involved ninety-nine complete virus sequences. The report also stated that the West African Ebola strain was absolutely different from the strain that had circulated in Central Africa in the 1970s. The study was done by geneticists at the Broad Institute of MIT and Harvard University who sequenced the virus found in seventy-eight patients treated at the Kenema Government Hospital in eastern Sierra Leone between May and June 2015. The study confirmed that the virus that created the 2014 outbreak in West Africa had been present in the region since 2004, ten years before the outbreak.

This means that the time and place of the 2014 West African outbreak cannot be located in the village of Miliandou in southeastern Guinea. But its genesis can be exactly situated in 2004 around the time of Dr. Aniru Conteh's death: the same year the United States/European funded biodefense research operations were instituted in the dilapidated hospital grounds of the Kenema Government Hospital in eastern Sierra Leone. The differences of the viral strain that most likely caused the West African outbreak from other known "Ebola strains in other African regions" could also possibly mean that the viral hemorrhagic fever that caused the outbreak itself may be associated with Lassa fever, which carries the same signs and symptoms as Ebola and Dengue fever: profuse vomiting, diarrhea, followed by bleeding, renal failure and cardiac arrest and then eventual death. Both Aniru Conteh, who died in 2004, and Sheikh Umar Khan, who died in 2014, experienced the same signs and symptoms before their deaths. And, oddly enough, they were both infected through similar circumstances: treating infected pregnant women at the Lassa Fever Ward of the Kenema Government Hospital.

The French medical charity, *Medicins Sans Frontiers* (MSF), in its evaluation of the causes of the widespread explosion of the Ebola outbreak, singled out Metabiota for criticism, accusing its staff deployed in Sierra Leone of withholding critical information that would have assisted in the reversal of the casualties of the epidemic during its initial stages of the outbreak. "From the onset of the epidemic, the US biotechnology company Metabiota and Tulane University, partners of Sierra Leone's Kenema hospital, had the lead in supporting Sierra Leone's Ministry of Health in investigating suspected cases. Their investigations came back Ebola-negative, while their ongoing surveillance activities seem to have missed the cases of Ebola that had emerged in the country," MSF stated in a report released a year into the outbreak.[105]

Indeed Metabiota, a member of the VHFC, has been a central player in the decade-old western research operations in Kenema that followed the CDC's reclassification of the Lassa virus as a threat agent against western security interests. Metabiota and Tulane University have been on the ground and were instrumental in the transformation of eastern Sierra Leone (Kenema Government Hospital) into an outpost of the United States war on terror through its *Diagnostics for Biodefense* project. So it is extremely possible that the post-war western medical research activities in eastern Sierra Leone, supported by millions of biodefense dollars for research on pathogenesis and genomics, directly contributed to the 2014 health catastrophe in West Africa. The fact that the 2014 West Africa epidemic unfolded at least ten years after the inauguration of the United States biodefense research project and only four years after the establishment of the VHFC in eastern Sierra Leone is clearly indicative of the burden of responsibility that these multilateral research operations have towards the outbreak. While the recalibration of Lassa as a regional and international security threat attracted millions of dollars from biodefense coffers for research organizations and scientists, West Africa's public health concerns were never prioritized in the biodefense research operations of the VHFC. The fact that the Kenema-Kailahun axis, considered a major component of the Lassa belt and hub of the many western funded biodefense research activities, became the epicenter of the 2014 outbreak in Sierra Leone sends a serious question about the actual motives of the United States and European biodefense concerns in West Africa.

The CDC's recalibration of Lassa as a potential bioweapon turned into a public health security risk for West Africa. But these security risks were embedded only within western security concerns and these efforts did not prevent the occurrence of the kind of outbreak whose risk had laid the foundation for biodefense investments and research in West Africa a decade earlier. The money that went into western laboratory research in Kenema did nothing to upgrade the health infrastructure in Sierra Leone or other parts of West Africa. The health situation in West Africa remained dilapidated despite the influx of millions of biodefense funds into the region.

For example, there was no thermometer at the Lassa Ward in Kenema right up to the 2014 outbreak despite the presence of western researchers and regardless of the fact that temperature readings are a key part of the case identification protocols for Lassa fever. A study done on the Kenema Lassa Ward a year before the 2014 outbreak revealed the stark absence of basic protective equipment like gloves for health care workers handling Lassa cases. Nurses at the Lassa Ward

---

[105] See MSF's report, "Pushed to the Limit and Beyond: A Year into the Largest Ever Ebola Outbreak" for a comprehensive summary of this question.

reportedly re-used needles on patients, which implied that needles were recapped, thereby increasing the risks of infection on health workers.[106] Local health units in remote villages in eastern Sierra Leone also complained of a lack of equipment to diagnose and take samples from suspected Lassa cases for onward submission to the Lassa Laboratory in Kenema. These conditions existed alongside the many western biodefense research activities that occurred in Kenema from 2009-2014. These biodefense research operations in Kenema were carried out in a highly risky and mainly unprotected environment. This is in sharp contrast to safety procedures in the United States where the Lassa virus studies are handled in bio-safety level-four-facilities. Researchers in such facilities are required to wear "space suits." These measures were never applied in Kenema. The Kenema protective measures only included goggles, gloves, and masks, which were always in short supply.

"Certainly we have less safety, less containment, but we do have the ability to do a lot more in the same amount of time," an American research scientist told the Reuters News Agency three years ahead of the 2014 outbreak.[107] The absence of the required safety and containment measures needed to handle a CDC classified high-level threat pathogen in a dilapidated hospital facility posed severe risks to innocent health workers and the larger community. It was obvious that western scientists and researchers working on Lassa at the Kenema Government Hospital placed the larger eastern communities of Sierra Leone, and by extension the entire sub-region, susceptible to the same anticipated pathogenic risks that necessitated the millions of dollars in biodefense research operations in eastern Sierra Leone in the first place.

It is therefore possible that the 2014 West African outbreak could have been the result of safety procedural violations that exposed both the health workers and the larger patient population to infectious risks at the Kenema Government Hospital, where a highly dangerous pathogen, according to CDC classification, was being handled. Or it could have been a deliberate result of the experimentation of a *weaponized version* of Lassa from the Kenema Lassa laboratory.

The fact that the 2014 outbreak occurred within the same geographical space hosting some of the leading western medical research institutions and major scientific groups from the United States and Europe renders the spontaneity theory of the 2014 epidemic absolutely baseless. To argue that the 2014 West African epidemic took the scientific world by surprise is a deliberate effort to exonerate and extricate the role of biodefense funding and western medical research from creating both the conditions for the epidemiological outbreak and simultaneously condoning its widespread transmission.

---

[106] Wilkinson, A., 'Lassa fever: The politics of an Emerging Disease and the Scope for One Health," STEPS Working Paper 83 (Brighton: STEPS Centre, 2015).

[107] Simon Akam, "U.S. Anti-terror Outpost Tackles Rat-borne Virus," *Reuters*, February 2011.

It will be difficult to extricate the role of the United States and European funded biomedical research operations in eastern Sierra Leone, which defined Lassa as a potential bioweapon, from the actual story surrounding the origin of the 2014 health epidemic in West Africa. The efforts of western scientists, the academic community, and its media representatives to situate the 2014 West African outbreak outside of the confines of the biomedical research projects at the Lassa Fever Laboratory of the Kenema Government Hospital in eastern Sierra Leone were clearly a deliberate narrative which sought to subsume the actual story surrounding the catastrophe that took place in the Mano River enclave of West Africa in 2014.

This fact is captured squarely by MSF in its evaluation of the international response to the epidemic. The MSF report which criticized Metabiota, Tulane University, and government officials in Sierra Leone for hindering its operations was not a simple criticism of national and international response mechanisms to an outbreak, but exposed significant false aspects of the mainstream narratives which now define the 2014 health tragedy in West Africa within western society.

MSF said Metabiota and health officials in Sierra Leone refused to release information relating to the contact lists of infected persons and kept all information about the outbreak in Sierra Leone to themselves. "When we set up operations in Kailahun, we realized we were already too late. There were cases everywhere", MSF stated. Why had Metabiota, Tulane University, or any of the other members of the VHFC who were engaged in the years-long study of Lassa's bioweapon's potential in Kenema failed to report the outbreak of the epidemic when it first occurred? Or why did they withhold all relevant information that would been instrumental in the battle against the outbreak?

These questions enter the heart of the outbreak: its place of origin and modes of transmission. At the initial stages of the outbreak, official records in Sierra Leone situated the epidemic in May 2014 on a traditional healer that had traveled to Guinea for a funeral, where it is claimed she was infected with the virus before returning to Sierra Leone in May. Recent evidence now confirms that the WHO and regional authorities in West Africa knew as early as February 2014 that infectious sick people in eastern Sierra Leone were migrating across the border into the southern region of Guinea – three months before the official narrative locates the virus in the country.

In particular, a patient named Sia Wanda Koniono from Kailahun had fallen sick and was said to have crossed into Guinea several times for medical treatment before she died. Individuals who were exposed to her in Guinea were later confirmed to have died of Ebola. An official report by a team of WHO experts and Guinean officials who had investigated the situation stated that authorities in Freetown and members of VHFC in Kenema had knowledge of Koniono's death from hemorrhagic fever, but they made no effort to trace the contacts that may have possibly been infected months ahead of the official declaration of the outbreak in Sierra Leone. MSF officials in Guinea disclosed that an e-mail attachment mentioning Koniono and other patients from Sierra Leone who were crossing into Guinea was sent to Dr. Sheik Umarr Khan in late March 2014, several weeks before Sierra Leone officially acknowledged the presence of the virus in the country. Reports alleged that neither Khan nor any of the VHFC members responded to the correspondences.[108]

"Ebola cases in Guinea were discovered that were reportedly coming from Sierra Leone," MSF stated in its report. This is the opposite of the official narrative, based on Leendertz's account, which claimed the virus moved from Guinea into Sierra Leone and then into Liberia. This fact also exposes the false narrative of the origin of the outbreak in Sierra Leone, both in terms of place and time, which earlier official records claimed was caused by an infected traditional healer's funeral. It is therefore obvious that the "zoonotic origin of the West African Ebola epidemic" advanced by Fabian Leendertz, which located the origin of the outbreak in Guinea, was not just the deliberate criminalization of the victims of a human-induced tragedy, but may also be part of intensive international efforts to cover-up the actual historic chain of events that laid the foundation for the outbreak. By so doing, Leendertz and his colleagues, in alliance with many in the western media, were exonerating the role of western biodefense funding and its international protagonists from responsibility for creating the actual causes of a disaster that claimed thousands of innocent lives in West Africa and inflicted irreparable damages to the region's socio-cultural fabric.

---

[108] Kevin Sack et al., "How Ebola Roared Back," *The New York Times*, 29 December 2014 (www.nytimes.com/2014/12/30/health/how-ebola-roared-back.html).

PART TWO
POLITICAL ECONOMY
OF THE EBOLA EPIDEMIC

CHAPTER 4

GLOBAL EBOLA RESPONSE: IMPERIALIST OPPORTUNISM, GEOPOLITICAL INTERESTS

Many of the member states here today have invested heavily in chemical and biological response. To curb the epidemic, it is imperative that states immediately deploy civilian and military assets with expertise in biohazard containment. I call upon you to dispatch your disaster response teams, backed by the full weight of your logistical capabilities. We cannot cut off the affected countries and hope this epidemic will simply burn out. To put out this fire, we must run into the burning building...

— Dr. Joanne Liu, MSF's International President[109]

The international military deployments which accompanied the 2014 outbreak in West Africa revealed a significant aspect of contemporary international relations: the new face of imperialism and the strategic significance of West Africa in the current geopolitical contest for territory and resource control by old and new global forces.

The call for military deployments, invited by MSF's international president Joanne Liu on September 2, 2014, came almost a month after the WHO declared the Ebola outbreak a public health emergency of international concern. Thousands of deaths occurred in the region and thousands more were being infected on a daily basis. A few weeks before this appeal, western television channels broadcasted images of dead bodies thrown on the streets of Monrovia in Liberia. Health workers were turning-away patients from treatment centers for lack of sufficient beds to admit new arrivals. At the ELWA Hospital, one of the largest treatment centers in Liberia, MSF staff could only open the gates for thirty

---

[109] *"Pushed to the Limit and Beyond: A Year into the Largest Ever Ebola Outbreak,"* MSF Report, March 2015.

minutes each morning to take in a few patients. New patients were admitted only after those who had died the previous night made the beds empty. Western television images showed how sick people died outside the gates of MSF treatment centers in Monrovia. One television reporter transmitted the story of a father who arrived with his daughter in the car's trunk at the ELWA Treatment Center, begging MSF staff to take her in to prevent the infection of his other children at home. The MSF staff turned the man and his daughter away. In another article, the reporter told the story of a woman cradling her infected five-year-old son, while her other ten-year old boy lay dead on the floor. The father of the two children died the previous night. They arrived at the ELWA Treatment Center seeking help but could not get in because the gates were closed.

"We had to make the horrendous decision of who we could let into the treatment center," Rosa Crestani, an MSF staff in Monrovia told the *Reuters News Agency* in Monrovia.[110]

In a desperate appeal for help, Jackson Naimah, the MSF's Team Leader in Liberia reported to the United Nations Security Council saying, "As I speak, people are sitting at the gates of our centers, literally begging for their lives. They rightly feel alone, neglected, denied – left to die a horrible, undignified death. We are failing the sick because there is not enough help on the ground."[111]

He hoped that his chilling appeal would convince global leaders in New York to Washington, London, Geneva, and Paris to act immediately and stem the spiraling tide of the daily exploding infections and horrendous deaths occurring in Liberia. At the beginning of the outbreak, MSF leaders in Europe and West Africa tried unsuccessfully to convince the international community about the severity of the unfolding crisis. MSF issued a public statement on March 31, 2014, describing the outbreak as "unprecedented," but WHO officials in Geneva objected to the MSF's declaration. They said the outbreak was not unprecedented and not different from previous outbreaks in the 1970s.[112] Regional political leaders in West Africa reinforced the WHO position. National authorities in Guinea and Sierra Leone dismissed the MSF declaration and accused its staff of causing public panic to drive away potential visitors and investors in the region. In Guinea, president Alpha Conde told journalists on May 10, 2014 that MSF was spreading panic because it wanted to raise funds for its operations. His counterparts in Sierra Leone allegedly refused MSF access to the contact lists of earlier infections and

---

[110] "Doctors without Borders Says Slow Ebola Response needlessly killed thousands," *Reuters*, March 23, 2015 (www.nydailynews.com/life-style/health/medical-charity-slow-ebola-response-killed-thousands-article-1.2159213).

[111] Jackson Naimah's statement to the United Nations Security Council meeting held in New York to discuss the security implication of the outbreak.

[112] "UN Health Agency Resisted Declaring Ebola Emergency," Associated Press, March 20, 2015 (www.nytimes.com/aponline/2015/03/20/world/ap-un-who-bunglingebola.html).

instructed that only laboratory-confirmed deaths were to be reported.[113]

A few weeks after these denials and accusations against MSF coming from international policy makers and regional leaders in Sierra Leone and Guinea, the outbreak forced itself into the global agenda. The epidemic claimed its first high profile casualties and threatened a spread across the Atlantic Ocean into Europe and the United States. First, Sierra Leone's leading virologist, Sheikh Umarr Khan, was infected and died in an MSF treatment center in Kailahun in late July. Then Patrick Sawyer, a forty-year-old Liberian-American consultant with the Liberian Ministry of Finance, collapsed upon arrival in Lagos, Nigeria for a conference and died five days later of Ebola. The doctor who treated Sawyer also died of Ebola a few days later. Nine other confirmed cases of Ebola infections and eight deaths were recorded in Nigeria. That same week, two American aid workers with Samaritan's Purse in Liberia also tested positive for Ebola and were evacuated to the United States for medical care. Then another man, Thomas Eric Duncan, who had returned from Liberia, tested positive for Ebola at a hospital in Dallas, Texas. Duncan's was the first diagnosed case outside of West Africa. A nurse in Spain who treated a Spanish citizen infected with Ebola tested positive for the virus. She became the first human-to-human transmission of Ebola in Europe.[114]

These high profile deaths and infections attracted global media attention and occupied the agenda of international policy leaders. Western hysteria, accentuated by the fear of a potential spread of the outbreak in Europe and America, reached its climax with these incidental cases that arrived in Europe and the United States. International recognition of the severity of the outbreak forcefully hit western society. International political leaders and their disease control specialists called the epidemic an international security threat. Ebola and the ISIS question competed for attention on the agenda of the White House and United States Department of Defense. At a meeting with the CDC in Atlanta on September 16, 2014, United States President Barrack Obama said, "This is an epidemic that is not just a threat to regional security. It's a potential threat to global security if these countries break down…(This) has profound effects on all of us, even if we are not directly contracting the disease."[115]

Obama's statement re-echoed comments made at a news conference a week earlier by Liberia's National Defense Minister, Brownie Samukai, who called the epidemic a serious threat to the country's national existence. His colleague,

[113] Colin, Freeman (2015) "Guinea and Sierra Leone tried to cover up Ebola crisis, says Medecins Sans Frontieres," *Telegraph*, March 23, 2015 (www.telegraph.co.uk/news/worldnews/ebola/11488726/Guinea-and-Sierra-Leone-tried-to-cover-up-Ebola-crisis-says-Medecins-Sans-Frontieres.html).

[114] "US Ebola patient Thomas Duncan Dies in Hospital," *BBC News Online*, October 8, 2014 (www.bbc.com/news/world-us-canada-29543956).

[115] Helene Cooper, et al., "U.S. to Commit Up to 3,000 Troops to Fight Ebola in Africa," *New York Times*, September 15, 2014 (www.nytimes.com/2014/09/16/world/africa/obama-to-announce-expanded-effort-against-ebola.html).

Finance Minister Amara Konneh told reporters two days later that Liberia was at war with an unknown enemy. "Liberia faces a serious threat to its national existence," Samukai told the United Nations Security Council in New York.

The gruesome deaths and spiraling infections in Liberia and Sierra Leone, in particular, disrupted everyday life in many of the affected communities. Community revolts were erupting regularly against government quarantine measures. National disease control laws passed by local authorities in a belated response to contain the outbreak affected individual freedoms and worsened people's daily lives. In Monrovia's West Point community, angry crowds broke the government's quarantine and stormed a nearby treatment center, looting beds and mattresses and releasing the patients housed within its walls. In the Kono and Kenema districts of eastern Sierra Leone, angry youths equally revolted against health care workers and attempted to burn down treatment centers alleging that Ebola was being spread deliberately. Police intervened in both instances and, in Kenema, police bullets injured a boy. News also emerged from southern Guinea that angry villagers attacked and killed a group of aid workers who had gone to the area to conduct community education campaigns about the epidemic.

Leaders of the affected countries immediately convened an extraordinary summit of the Mano River Union presidents in Conakry on August 1, 2014, to discuss the unfolding protests and the epidemic. They issued a Joint Declaration imposing cross-border isolation zones and national restrictions on public gatherings and free movement. "We have agreed to take important and extraordinary actions at the inter country level to focus on cross-border regions that have more than seventy percent of the epidemic. Police and the military will isolate these areas," they said in the Joint Declaration.[116] The Conakry meeting ended with an appeal to Barrack Obama to include the Ebola outbreak on the agenda of his US-Africa Leaders Summit in Washington that was to be held a week later. The presidents of Sierra Leone and Liberia were forced into absence at the meeting by the exploding epidemic and its accompanying revolts.

In Washington, Obama announced the deployment of a United States military force of 3,000 troops in Monrovia to be commanded by Major General Darryl A. Williams, Commander of the United States Army's Africa Command (AFRICOM). "We're going to establish a military command center in Liberia to support civilian efforts across the region. It's going to be commanded by Major General Darryl Williams, commander of our Army forces in Africa," US president, Barrack Obama announced on September 16, 2014, at the CDC headquarters in Atlanta. Following Obama's statement, Defense Department officials called on Congress to re-allocate more than US$500 million in military spending for the

---

[116] Cholo Brooks, "Mano River Union Leaders Agree On Measures To Fight Ebola". *Global News Network*, August 4, 2014 (www.gnnliberia.com/articles/2014/08/04/mano-river-union-leaders-agree-measures-fight-ebola).

West African military deployment. This was in addition to Obama's request for an approval of US$30 million from Congress to dispatch additional response workers, laboratory supplies, and equipment. The overall United States military deployment in West Africa, code named "Operation United Assistance," was estimated to cost around US$750 million over a six month period. Barely two weeks after the announcement, US military forces arrived in Monrovia and commenced deployment. In London, British Foreign Secretary Philip Hammond also announced the United Kingdom's plan to deploy 750 British military personnel into Sierra Leone. The UK's military force in Sierra Leone comprised of 250 troops on the Royal Fleet Auxiliary ship, RFA Argus stationed on the coastline of Freetown, three fighter helicopters, and 500 ground troops. British officials said £125 million (over US$200 million) was committed to the British response operations in Sierra Leone. By early November 2014 nearly all of the international countries involved in the Ebola response efforts in West Africa, with the exception of Cuba, had established a heavy military presence in West Africa. These new military deployments were in addition to existing French military presence in Mali and the Central Africa Republic, and in addition to over a decade-old British military base in Freetown, the International Security Advisory Team (ISAT). Apart from western military forces, China, for the first time, also deployed a detachment of the Chinese Liberation Army in Sierra Leone.[117]

Race for African Resources in the Twenty-first Century

Were these rapid international military deployments in West Africa actually in response to the exploding health crisis? Or was the international military response, invoked by western nations, a smokescreen to cover-up current twenty-first century military ambitions aimed at protecting the economic and geopolitical interests of global market forces and their governments? Most importantly, did international military deployments actually help in containing the exploding Ebola outbreak?

These questions are central to understanding the significance of West Africa in the current global contest between western capitalist nations and the emerging economic giants of Asia led by China. West Africa remains an area of strategic significance to global market forces and several western governments. France, the United States, and Britain's centuries of colonial relationships with the area are still factors in the economic and political arrangements that take place in the region. The Mano River countries of Liberia, Sierra Leone, and Guinea host some of the world's leading multinationals and corporate giants, owned largely

[117] "Ebola outbreak: Britain sending 750 soldiers and medics to Western Africa," *The Independent*, September 8, 2015 (www.independent.co.uk/life-style/health-and-families/health-news/ebola-outbreak-britain-sends-750-soldiers-and-medics-to-western-africa-9783010.html). Also see, for additional information, Thomas Gaist, "US-NATO War Games Prepare Massive Military Escalation in West Africa," *World Socialist*, 2015 Web. February 17, 2015 (https://www.wsws.org/en/articles/2015/02/17/boko-f17.html).

by European and North American capitalist corporations and multinationals. The burden to protect the economic activities of these corporations remains at the heart of the United States and European foreign policy relations with the countries in the region.

The three countries – Sierra Leone, Liberia and Guinea – have some of the world's largest deposits of iron ore, bauxite, aluminum, diamonds, gold, and other environmental resources. In Liberia, for instance, Firestone, a US-owned rubber company, and the Liberian-American Mining Company (LAMCO), a Rio Tinto iron-ore conglomerate, have dominated the exploitation of rubber and iron ore resources from Liberia for over a hundred years. American and European corporations have dominated the mining and environmental resource exploitation activities in the Mano River enclave (the heart of the 2014 Ebola outbreak) since the 1930s. The transitions from direct colonial rule to "African self-government" in the 1950s and 1960s only increased the monopolization of the natural resources of the region. Colonial era corporations and multinationals assumed new names and "indigenized management boards" but maintained the established chains of resource exploitation and international finance transfers over the decades. A new trend of "corporate colonialism" thrived in West Africa with the arrival of local political elites in power following the departure of white colonialist officials and the assumption of new flags and new national anthems. These indigenous political elites, usually propped to power through vote rigging and western campaign finance, represent mostly the political and economic interests of Europe and America. The end of the West African civil wars of the 1990s, however, introduced a new trend in the pattern of "corporate colonialism" in the region: the shift towards land grabbing by new European agricultural corporations and the recent threats posed by new corporate arrivals from China.

The arrival of Chinese corporations in Africa, driven by China's growing demands for oil, minerals, and environmental resources to feed its rising industrialized economy, presents a serious challenge to western corporate monopoly interests in West Africa. Over the last twenty years, China has turned Africa into a supplier of natural resources and also a destination for China's new export markets. African governments, jolted by IMF/World Bank conditions over the decades, now see China as an alternative in the international geopolitical and economic environment. China's economic deals with African governments are free from the usual demands for political reforms that come with western finance capital. Angered by African governments' willingness to provide China unfettered access to the continent's mineral and energy resources, Europe and the United States allege that China bankrolls corrupt and repressive regimes in Africa. Chinese officials have responded that Washington and its European allies are not actually concerned with human rights and democratic issues, but highlight such issues in order to constrain China's economic programs and growing influence in Africa. At the back of these western criticisms of China, however, is the hidden fear by the United States that China's increased economic activities will eventually translate into active military deployments in Africa.[118] These western fears are, however, not unfounded. In October 2014, China concluded negotiations for the establishment of a military base in the port of Djibouti, a territory hosting the largest American military deployment in Africa and used by United States Special Forces for covert operations in Yemen and other parts of Africa. France and Japan, two leading allies of the United States, equally rely on the port of Djibouti, located at the entrance of the Red Sea and the Suez Canal, to fight off pirates in nearby Somalia. Early in 1998, a military commission established by China's Peoples Liberation Army advised Chinese officials on the need to increase arms sales to Africa and establish strategic military training programs for selected countries in order to counter the United States and other Western military programs on the continent.[119]

A recent study in the United States done by the Center for the Study of Chinese Military Affairs at the National Defense University observed that China's expanding international economic interests are likely to generate increasing demands for its military operations. The study noted that China's rapidly expanding international interests will produce a parallel expansion of its navy operations in a bid to protect Chinese citizens, investments, and sea lines of communication. In addition to navy operations, Chinese international expansion means that China would have to establish direct military bases in Africa if it is to ably protect Chinese investments and economic interests.[120]

China's increased interest in Africa coincided with the United States (Bush administration) strategic re-evaluation of the continent as a potential energy reserve and a secure alternative for petroleum resources rather than the Middle East where western corporate interests face continued resistance. It was this economic re-prioritization of Africa that produced the proposal for the US African Command (AFRICOM), a new military base to be located on African soil. This move was largely believed to be a direct response to growing Chinese economic influence, and the rising fears in Washington that China's future military ambitions in Africa would affect its strategic interests. In fact, the announcement of the AFRICOM plan was made the same week that Chinese president Hu Jintao was completing an African tour in 2006.[121]

This United States re-prioritization of the alternative viability of Africa's

---

[118] Lafargue, F. "China's Presence in Africa," *China Perspectives*, No. 61, (September- October 2005) p. 2.

[119] "Historic Chinese military base to open in Horn of Africa," *RFI*, May 11, 2015.

[120] Yung, Christopher D., Rustici, R. (2014) "Not an Idea We Have to Shun: Chinese Overseas Basing Requirements in the 21st Century," Center for the Study of Chinese Military Affairs, National Defense University: China Strategic Perspectives, No. 7, NDU Press, October 2014.

[121] "President Bush Creates a Department of Defense Unified Combatant Command for Africa," *NPR Morning Edition*, February 6, 2007, Georgewbush-whitehouse.archives.gov, Web. 19 May 2015. See also, Northham, Jackie, "Pentagon Creates Military Command for Africa," February 7, 2007, Web. 25 June 2015.

energy resource potentials elevated the strategic significance of the continent not only on its national security agenda, but also on that of China's as well. The United States and China's contending economic re-prioritization of Africa for its natural wealth has created a "silent superpower rivalry" for control of geopolitical frontiers and economic resources on the continent.

In 2008 when the United States was still struggling to convince African governments to accept the proposed deployment of AFRICOM on African soil, China, on the other hand, had already deployed three navy warships in the Gulf of Aden as part of its efforts to secure its own economic interests in Africa. While China made easy progress with establishing military presence in Africa (including a contribution of more than 500 troops to the UN Mission in Liberia), the United States' proposal to deploy AFRICOM on African soil received severe criticisms and negative responses from African governments. African opposition to AFRICOM grew exponentially throughout 2007 and 2008, owing mainly to the outcome of the 2003 US-led invasion of Iraq and the 2006-2007 US-backed Ethiopian invasion of Somalia. Although the United States was able to reach an agreement with Liberia for the use of its territory for AFRICOM's deployment, this proved difficult to actualize because of persistent criticisms against large-scale US military deployment in the region.

While the question of AFRICOM remained unresolved since its conception, China, however, made significant inroads in securing major energy deals and mining concessions across Africa, and was doing so successfully in areas of strategic interests to the United States. In Sudan, for instance, China's National Petroleum Corporation (CNPC) is now the single largest shareholder (controlling over 40 percent) in the Greater Nile Petroleum Operating Company, which controls Sudan's oil fields. Over the last decade China has invested a total of US$3 billion in refinery and pipeline construction. In West Africa, Petro China, one of the leading Chinese oil companies, concluded an US$800 million deal with the Nigerian National Petroleum Corporation to purchase 30,000 barrels of crude oil per day for a period of one year in 2005. The following year, China's National Offshore Oil Corporation (CNOOC), after failing to acquire the American-owned Unocal, purchased a forty-five percent stake in a Nigerian offshore oil and gas field for US$2.27 billion with a promise to invest an additional US$2.25 billion in field development. China has also infiltrated every facet of the economic and political environment of Liberia, a United States colonial territory with immense strategic significance to American geo-economic and political interests in Africa. Chinese construction companies and mining corporations are taking over significant concessionary rights both in Liberia and Sierra Leone previously controlled by American and British corporations and multinationals.[122]

---

[122] Bezlova, "China's Soft-Power Diplomacy in Africa," *Asia Times*, June 23, 2006 (www.atimes.com/atimes/China/HF23Ad01.html).

The China Union Investment Company, a Monrovia-based affiliate of the China Union Mining, was awarded the Bong Iron Mines concession in 2009 for a twenty-five year period with exploration rights limited to five years. Other leading Chinese corporations in Liberia include China Henan International Cooperation Group, China Chongqing International Construction Corporation, Qing Dao Construction Group, Riders Incorporated, and Vic Liberia Development Corporation; all are engaged in large-scale mining operations, oil exploration, and huge road construction. China also dominates infrastructure and construction projects and iron ore mining in Sierra Leone. China's Shandong Steel Company, which initially owned less than a fifty percent interest in the British-supported African Minerals of Frank Timis, is now the exclusive concessionary owner of one of West Africa's largest iron deposits located in northern Sierra Leone.

Real motives for international military deployments

How did this contending race for geopolitical and economic frontiers between the Euro-American alliance and China influence the military approach of the international response to the 2014 outbreak in West Africa? And how did the growing security anxieties of the United States and China, created mainly by superpower rivalries over economic interests, contribute to the widespread explosion of the epidemic?

In a report evaluating the international response to the outbreak, MSF said the militarized response did not include deployment of sufficient qualified and trained medical staffs to treat patients on the ground. MSF was disappointed that majority of the military efforts deployed in October and November was limited mostly to operational support for international aid organizations and local political authorities. "There was a clear reluctance to jump in and care for patients. US helicopters would not even transport laboratory samples or health personnel returning from treating patients," Joanne Liu, MSF's International President said.[123]

MSF said its appeal for international military deployments were based on the recognition that the epidemic would not be brought to a halt by international aid organizations alone but required the intervention of military units with some level of biological warfare expertise. International military troops were indeed deployed but MSF said the request for the deployment of biohazard teams was never met. The foreign military arrivals only built medical facilities to treat local and foreign health care workers but they provided no direct personal care to affected communities. MSF was not alone in its criticism of the militarized approach of the international response to the epidemic. Civil society groups and residents of affected communities in Sierra Leone also criticized the effectiveness of British military response to the outbreak.

---

[123] "Push to the Limit and Beyond," *MSF Report.*

The criticisms came after an astronomical increase in infections and death numbers the weeks following the British deployments in Sierra Leone. WHO reported over two thousand new infections during the last three weeks of November. This was two times the official number of infections in Guinea and Liberia combined. In the first week of December, almost a hundred new infections were recorded in a single day. These astronomical increases were occurring unabatedly, despite the presence of British military intervention in the country. Towards the end of December 2014 when Sierra Leone led the charts on new infections and deaths, local newspapers in Freetown and community leaders questioned the essence of British military presence in Sierra Leone. The *Standard Times* newspaper in Freetown accused British troops of holding beer parties on the beaches of Freetown instead of helping to contain the outbreak.[124] British officials denied the press accusations saying that British soldiers deployed in Sierra Leone were only building new treatment centers and training medical personnel and were are not allowed even a beer.

These criticisms were not only directed against the effectiveness of the pattern of the international response but were by themselves direct interrogations of the actual motives surrounding the use of international military forces by western nations in humanitarian relief efforts, crisis management, and conflict resolution in Africa and other parts of the global south. The pattern and style of the 2014 western military deployments in West Africa were not only a re-perpetuation of the old nineteenth century colonial carve-up of Africa, but they also marked the effective re-actualization of renewed colonial ambitions necessitated by the rapidly changing realities of the current international economic and political landscape. For the United States, the military response was a direct fulfillment of its long-term plans to establish AFRICOM on the continent, especially so in West Africa where its interests are increasingly being challenged by growing Chinese economic activities. The epidemic provided the United States a *free pass* to actualize its twenty-first military ambitions in Africa: the deployment of thousands of US soldiers on African soil without any criticism from any sector of the anti-war movement or global peace organizations.

Therefore, it is clear that the international military deployments carried out in West Africa in response to the 2014 outbreak were not actually targeted to halt the exploding epidemic. They were largely motivated by international security concerns for the protection of local regimes against possible civil unrest, and the security and reclamation of strategic economic areas of interests. The three most-affected countries in West Africa had announced the discovery of new petroleum resources two years before the outbreak, a development that intensified renewed superpower rivalries over concessionary acquisitions. The humanitarian

---

[124] Andrew Harding, "Sierra Leone foreign Ebola relief operation criticized" November 30, 2014 (www.bbc.com/news/world-africa-30267600) Web 15 May 2015.

aspect of the outbreak was used as a smokescreen by superpower nations to fulfill twenty-first century militarily ambitions. For the United States and Europe, it marked the climax of its decade old West African security project, which invested millions of dollars in biodefense funding on pathogenic research and anti-terror campaign. Although a major outcome of the epidemic has been the convenient creation of multiple international military bases in West Africa, its origin cannot equally be divorced from the very international security concerns that turned the most affected countries into a site for biodefense research and investments. The contending geopolitical and economic interests of global powers – the United States, Britain, France, and China – in Africa, which resulted in the deployment of thousands of assorted military forces in West Africa, is surely the prelude to future events that would create the next round of conflicts and humanitarian crises in West Africa. The resource rich Mano River countries of Liberia, Sierra Leone, and Guinea, now defined by constant crises and deadly disease outbreaks, have been strategically carved-up for such a confrontation. Whether this anticipated confrontation will occur within the next decade is still uncertain, but what is obvious is the fact that the ongoing antagonistic competition between the United States and China for control of Africa's resources will eventually produce the region's next disastrous catastrophe and political nightmare.

CHAPTER 5

EBOLA HUMANITARIANISM: AID OR PROFIT?

Global wealth is increasingly being concentrated in the hands of a small wealthy elite. These wealthy individuals have generated and sustained their vast riches through their interests and activities in a few important economic sectors, including finance, pharmaceuticals and health care...
– Oxfam, *Wealth: Having It All And Wanting More (2015 Report)*[125]

On February 17, 2015, the *Concord Times* newspaper in Freetown published an alarming front-page story headlined "President Koroma Urges International Accountability of Ebola Funds.*"[126]* In the story, Koroma called on international organizations to account for the millions of dollars they had received on behalf of Sierra Leone for the fight against Ebola.

His statement came a week after a national audit stated that Koroma's government could not account for over a third of the national Ebola budget. An 84-page report released by the Sierra Leone Audit Service, which covered the first six months of the national Ebola response, discovered that over US$5 million allegedly spent on public procurements for ambulances, construction of a treatment center and other logistics could not be substantiated. The audit report put the Koroma government under severe criticisms by local and international media over its handling of the outbreak. In Sierra Leone, the audit scandal followed persistent accusations that national authorities were using the epidemic to enrich themselves. Some in the international community said the audit scandal was evidence of why the several millions of dollars sent to international organizations engaged in the Ebola response could not be handed directly to the Koroma

---

[125] "Wealth: Having it all and Wanting More," OXFAM's Issue Briefing Paper: p.1, January 2015.

[126] Alusine Sesay, "President Koroma urges international accountability of Ebola funds". *Concord Times*, February 17, 2015 (slconcordtimes.com/pres-koroma-urges-intl-accountability-of-ebola-funds).

government.

"We would not only limit (the accountability demand) to local players because the bulk of the Ebola funds that were taken for and on behalf of the people of this country were channeled through international NGOs and others. We are also going to demand equal transparency and accountability from the international community," Ernest Koroma responded to his international friends as he spoke at an event in Freetown held by the Sierra Leone Investment and Export Promotion Agency (SLIEPA) to discuss a post-Ebola economic recovery program for the country.[127]

Koroma's statement was a direct response to the criticism he was facing for the corruption that surrounded his national response to the outbreak. His statement raised a fundamental issue: the actual motives of international humanitarianism. To what extent can international organizations, involved in disaster response and crisis management, be held to account for the millions of dollars they raise in the name of helping victims of crises and disasters?

Humanitarian Opportunism and Failures in Sierra Leone

During the war years in the 1990s, the influx of international organizations in the country changed the character of Sierra Leone's cash-based economy. The influx of foreign aid workers meant a sporadic circulation of foreign currencies in the country. The results became unbearable on the local population: landlords charged exorbitant rent payments in dollar amounts, a near relegation of the national currency occurred and inflation digits climbed uncontrollably. The experience of the war years left an unbearable legacy about international aid and its work force: almost everyone in Sierra Leone, and much of the crisis-prone countries in the region, have not forgotten how the international funding that came during the civil war years was also taken away by the international staff who accompanied the donations.

In the wake of the West African outbreak, various governments and other private philanthropies donated over US$3 billion dollars to the Ebola response. But the funds were largely sent to western international aid organizations. Many of these international organizations are not strangers to the region. They were involved in the aid operations and humanitarian work during the civil wars in the 1990s. They departed from the region fifteen years ago when the wars were declared ended. They returned in 2014 with their usual four-wheel drive convoy, contending for space in the humanitarian field created by the outbreak. The staff of these international organizations got a monthly hazard pay of US$1600 and annual salaries between US$153,825 to US$187,904, depending on their rank in the system. Sierra Leone and the two other affected countries in the region were

---

[127] *NERC* press report on February 17, 2015.
(nerc.sl/?q=president-ernest-koroma-urges-international-accountability-ebola-funds).

witnesses to the lavish spending attitude of international humanitarian staff.[128]

In late September of 2014, the United Nations Secretary-General, Ban Ki-moon, announced the establishment of the United Nations Mission for Ebola Emergency Response (UNMEER) in Ghana. This was a few days after the UN Security Council declared the outbreak a threat to international security. The WHO officials stated that a total of US$490 million was needed to halt the transmission of Ebola in the affected countries within a nine-month period. A week later, the WHO's projected budget was increased to US$600 million. The United States gave US$423 million of its Ebola response money to the Centers for Disease Control (CDC) in Atlanta. The British also pledged a total of £205 million budget for its response. And the European Union added another €500 million. The same troops of aid forces, who departed the region after the war years, instantly re-surfaced in 2014.[129] The assortment of over a hundred non-governmental organizations immediately deployed their aid troops in Sierra Leone. The European Union alone sent about two thousand personnel into West Africa. Each of these organizations struggled for a piece of the millions of aid dollars announced by various governments and independent philanthropies.

Aid workers arrived in West Africa in a much-more lavish environment than during the war years. In Freetown, the United States Agency for International Development (USAID) booked all standard rooms at the Radisson Blu, a five star hotel on the coastline of Freetown, for a cost of US$270 per night over a six-month period. All business suites in that hotel cost US$350 a night. International aid workers said the Ebola crisis required expensive security measures: new four wheel drives, newly built hotels with air conditioned rooms in the affluent west-end of Freetown, and modern communication equipment; all this meant that more than half of the aid budget would go towards the upkeep of the international workforce that constantly arrived in the country.

While these troops of international aid workers flooded the region and occupied the many air-conditioned conference rooms and offices in Freetown, Conakry, and Monrovia, in the countryside local health workers who were in direct contact with infected persons and those involved in Ebola burials starved, going months without salaries, failing to receive even their meager weekly hazard payments of US$115. A *Newsweek* article, published in May 2015, documented tragic stories about local health workers involved in the fight against the outbreak. It reported testimonies of how local doctors, nurses, hospital cleaners, lab technicians, and burial workers went months without payments, tossed around within an

---

[128] Amy Maxmen, "Frontline health workers were sidelined in $3.3bn fight against Ebola". *Newsweek*, May 19, 2015 (europe.newsweek.com/frontline-health-workers-were-sidelined-3-3bn-fight-against-ebola-327485).

[129] See Amy Maxmen's Newsweek article "Frontline health workers were sidelined in $3.3bn fight against Ebola," of May 19, 2015 (www.newsweek.com/fight-against-ebola-front-line-health-workers-were-sidelined-funding-333436).

unnecessary bureaucracy created by exploitative international organizations and national authorities.

A US$23 million budget meant to address risk payments to local frontline workers was mismanaged with serious controversy and corruption. Protests by frontline workers over non-payments of health workers weekly risk allowances featured constantly throughout the outbreak. These protests continued while international aid workers travelled constantly on a United Nations helicopter across the country at an estimated cost of US$5,000 per trip. In total, the international humanitarian staff spent almost US$100 million on air travel in Sierra Leone alone.[130]

International policy makers in London, Paris, Brussels, Geneva, Washington, and New York were aware that the millions of dollars funneled into the Ebola response in West Africa were misappropriated and misdirected. A senior British official, Margaret Hodge revealed a disturbing reality during the middle of the outbreak: out of a €53 million European Union budget for frontline workers in Liberia, only €3.4 million actually reached local workers in the frontlines.[131] The Ebola funds had only created high paying jobs for international aid workers and opened incentives for local corruption to flourish, all at the expense of local health workers who faced the actual dangers of the outbreak.

Towards the end of November 2014, the WHO reported that over 622 health workers in West Africa were infected with the Ebola virus and 346 of that figure had died.[132] In December, the story of West Africa's Ebola frontline workers reached its apex in the western media: *Time* magazine named Ebola fighters its 2014 *Person of the Year.*[133] But what was absent in this glamorized heroism of frontline health workers in western media was the story of how their conditions helped raised funds that went only into the accounts of international aid organizations and local politicians.

In some ways, the stories of local health officials in West Africa resurrected the sad dual tragedy of the thousands of war amputees scattered across Sierra Leone today. Towards the end of the 1990s, images of Sierra Leone's amputees

---

[130] Amy Maxmen, "In Fight Against Ebola, Front-Line Health Workers Risked Their Lives And Never Got Paid," *Newsweek*, May 19, 2015 (www.newsweek.com/fight-against-ebola-front-line-health-workers-were-sidelined-funding-333436).

[131] Judith Ugwumadu, "MPs criticize DFID's slow response to Ebola," *Public Finance International*, February 10, 2015 (www.publicfinanceinternational.org/news/2015/02/mps-criticise-dfid's-'slow'-response-ebola). The Public Accounts Committee of the British Parliament stated in a report that the Department for International Development's (DFID) response to the Ebola epidemic in West Africa was too slow and failed to respond with urgency to the emerging crisis. It quoted Margaret Hodge who stated that had DFID reacted sooner, both lives and money might have been saved. Hodge was the chair of the Public Accounts Committee at the time of the outbreak.

[132] WHO's Monthly Ebola Report for November 2015.

[133] See "Why Ebola Fighters are TIME's Person of the Year 2014?" *Time Magazine*, December 10, 2014 (time.com/time-person-of-the-year-ebola-fighters-choice).

occupied front-pages of global newspapers and magazines. Global media beamed images of hacked limbs on western television to demonstrate the horrific brutality of wars and the extent of the humanitarian crisis they created. The United Nations and its chain of international aid organizations mobilized hundreds of millions of dollars in response to the catastrophe. The largest international military mission in the UN's history was deployed in Sierra Leone in the 1990s. International policy makers rolled out a multi-million dollar resettlement and rehabilitation program in the country to repair the damage caused by the war. But the funds never reached the victims of the war. The United Nations spent several millions of dollars in a transitional justice program to punish key perpetrators of the atrocities. A tribunal structure that cost over US$2 million to build was set-up in Freetown for the trial. However, the victims of the atrocities for whom justice was sought were left in sub-human conditions across amputee camps around the country with no proper housing and health facilities.[134]

Foreign Aid and Underdevelopment

The underdevelopment that predated the war and the sufferings it created were never addressed as part of the agenda of the international intervention. When the multinational military force and its multitude of aid bureaucrats departed the country, they left behind a seriously ruined nation without basic social and economic development. The millions of dollars in aid and donor finance did not solve the pressing social and infrastructural needs of the country. The aid money generated through the deplorable images of war amputees and other victims was largely spent to upkeep the multinational military force and its battalion of international aid workers. At the time when the international military and aid forces departed, Sierra Leone ranked at the bottom of the human development index with the most horrible health statistics in the world. The huge tribunal complex in Freetown, built out of the aid dollars to punish key leaders of the war, was the only physical structure left behind by the previous multinational aid force that occupied the country towards the end of the 1990s. In 2014, this UN-built structure became the headquarters of the National Ebola Response Center (the agency leading the national response efforts in Sierra Leone).

Billions of dollars were donated in response to the 2014 outbreak in West Africa, but the international aid intervention, similar to the approach of the 1990s, only focused on outreach, public education, mass diagnosis, contact tracing, vaccine development, and clinical trials. Hundreds of millions of dollars were spent on community education campaigns, construction of make-shift holding

---

[134] Sulakshana Gupta, "The not so Special Court for Sierra Leone," *The New Internationalist Magazine*, Issue 427, November 1, 2009 (newint.org/columns/essays/2009/11/01/special-court-sierra-leone). See also, for additional illustration, Celina Schocken's, "The Special Court for Sierra Leone: Overview and Recommendations," *Berkeley J. Int'l Law*, 20 No. 436 (2002) Available at: scholarship.law.berkeley.edu/bjil/vol20/iss2/3.

centers and treatment facilities made-with tarpaulin, transportation services, logistics, salaries, and on similar programs. All of these temporal projects eventually disappeared again as the crisis dissipated. The international aid force that had left behind dilapidated health centers and hospitals with poor service infrastructure in the 1990s returned in 2014 into the same environment. Today, with billions of dollars already spent in the international response efforts, the international aid work force has built no permanent hospitals or health centers in any of the three most affected countries. This international aid workforce will eventually depart West Africa, the same way they did in the 1990s, leaving behind the same chronic health infrastructure incapable of preventing an outbreak from becoming an epidemic. Evidence of the millions of dollars of aid money will endure only as tales told by victims and survivors of the deadly outbreak.

CHAPTER 6

POLITICAL CORRUPTION, STATE REPRESSION AND THE EBOLA RESPONSE

Monies that have been set aside for the purpose of combating the Ebola outbreak may have been used for unintended purposes, thereby slowing the government's response to eradicate the virus...
— Sierra Leone Audit Service[135]

On the morning of April 19, 2015, reports emerged in Freetown that ten people – all of them opposition party activists – were arrested from their various homes across the city. The arrests followed a massive police raid in response to a youth protest that occurred three days earlier at the gates of the United Sates Embassy in Freetown. The ten arrested individuals were allegedly part of a group of youths who stood at the gates of the United States Embassy on the morning of August 16, 2015, with placards to protest against Ernest Koroma's handling of the Ebola outbreak. They were allegedly angry that the national Ebola response was clouded by massive state corruption and the president's abuse of national constitutional provisions.[136]

The protest itself occurred a day after a meeting between Barrack Obama and the presidents of Sierra Leone, Liberia, and Guinea (the most affected countries) in Washington during the 2015 IMF/World Bank spring meetings. At the said meeting, Obama praised the three presidents' national response mechanisms to combat the outbreak. He said they demonstrated exceptional leadership in the fight against corruption and the Ebola outbreak. The Obama statement appeared

---

[135] Sierra Leone Audit Service Report on Ebola Funds covering the first six months of the outbreak.

[136] "SLPP Youth Demo In Freetown," *Global Times*, Freetown, April 17, 2015 (www.globaltimes-sl.com/slpp-youth-demo-in-freetown).

to have directly angered citizens of Sierra Leone and Guinea. The statement, which openly endorsed the leadership of the three presidents, deliberately ignored the prevailing public moods in Sierra Leone and Guinea. Weeks before this event, a campaign of sustained national protests ensued in Sierra Leone and Guinea against undemocratic practices of these national leaders and their poor handling of the Ebola outbreak. In Conakry, for example, opposition political parties were staging violent protests in the city over the president's lack of willingness to implement an elections timetable. And in Freetown, a national audit on Ebola funds reported that public officials affected the Ebola fight by stealing more than a third of the donated funds for the outbreak. In fact, Koroma had unconstitutionally dismissed the elected vice president of Sierra Leone just a few weeks before his Washington trip. These incidents created intense political moments across Sierra Leone and beyond. In Europe and America, Sierra Leoneans held massive demonstrations against Koroma demanding the reinstatement of the sacked vice president and prosecution of individuals accused of stealing Ebola funds.

The multiple demonstrations held mainly in London, Washington DC, and New York aimed to draw the attention of international policy leaders on the unfolding corruption and constitutional violations that surrounded the Ebola response efforts in Sierra Leone. But the several protests appeared to have been ignored by global political leaders. In the case of Sierra Leone, the United States Embassy in Freetown turned down an asylum request from Sierra Leone's vice president a few days before he was dismissed by Koroma for his reported ambitions to succeed the president. His asylum was denied despite the deployment of armed men to his home by the Koroma administration. State Department officials in Freetown claimed that the conflicting parties should utilize the national legal framework available in the country for redress. With the Obama statement, however, it appeared that the United States had publicly backed Koroma's government despite the escalating national and international demonstrations by Sierra Leoneans.

Neocolonialism and Authoritarian Democracy in Sierra Leone

Koroma came to power in 2007 through controversial elections that were allegedly marred by corrupt electoral management: over 477 polling stations in the predominant base of his opponent (an incumbent party candidate) were unprecedentedly excluded from the general vote count by the Sierra Leone National Electoral Commission (NEC), a factor that gave Koroma an undue advantage in the presidential race. Leading representatives of the United Nations missions stationed in Sierra Leone at the time were accused of having aided Ernest Koroma in the alleged electoral malpractice that brought him to power in 2007.[137]

The leading contender to Koroma's candidacy petitioned his victory in the

---

[137] Solomon E. Berewa, "A New Perspective On Governance, Leadership, Conflict And Nation Building In Sierra Leone," (London: Author House, UK, 2011).

Sierra Leone Supreme Court, challenging the validity of the votes. Regardless of the Supreme Court petition and protests against his questionable electoral victory, Koroma's ascension to power was overtly supported and hailed by Britain, the United States, and numerous western multinational corporations engaged in the decades of resource exploitation in the country. Immediately after the elections, the British Department for International Development (DFID), who had withheld donor funding to the previous government, announced that England was providing some US$72 million to support Koroma's "new economic reform program."

Douglas Alexander, Britain's Secretary of State for International Development, revealed that the fund was a new British assistance to help Koroma implement policies that would "maximize revenue" as part of a new national agenda. The said national agenda referred to Koroma's corporatist program: a neoliberal program that aimed to enhance western corporate monopoly over land, minerals, and energy resources through policy enactments or reforms that offered a range of favorable guarantees and tax incentives to western investment capital. When he came to power, Koroma, an insurance broker, announced that he would pursue an aggressive business plan: transforming Sierra Leone into an investment destination for large-scale multinational capital holdings on diamonds, iron ore, bauxite, petroleum, and other extractive industries. He told the British business and political class at Chatham House in London (formerly the Royal Institute for International Affairs) that his government would run Sierra Leone as a business, putting every sector of the country on auction to corporate bidding – obtaining "profit" and "capital regeneration" in exchange for natural resources.

To implement his new business plan, Koroma hired former British Prime Minister Tony Blair as his international lobbyist and public relations campaigner. Blair established a desk of his Africa Governance Initiative at the State House in Freetown and operated a multi-million dollar budget from Sierra Leonean taxpayer funds. To promote Koroma's new market investment agenda, Blair branded Sierra Leone a bastion of stable democracy. An investment conference in London, convened with Blair's efforts in late 2009, billed the country as a destination for endless marketing opportunities conducive for international financial investments. The International Finance Corporation (IFC) funded a reform of Sierra Leone's investment climate. The Sierra Leone Investment and Export Promotion Agency (SLIEPA) was formed to ease the burden of doing business in the country mainly for western business ventures. A year later in 2008, the IFC, in its annual doing business report, ranked Sierra Leone as one of the leading destinations for safe and easy-to-do-business countries. The Blair campaign eventually culminated into a flood of so-called foreign direct investments in the country's natural resources. British and other European corporations and multinational financial organizations immediately arrived in Sierra Leone to acquire concessionary holdings in the iron ore and petroleum resources.

By 2011, some of these multinationals had acquired more than 500,000 hectares of farmland in Sierra Leone. Addax Bioenergy of Switzerland, Quifel Natural Resources of Portugal, CAPARO Renewable Agricultural Developments of England, and Sepahan Afrique of Iran, the new agribusiness corporations who had taken over farmlands in the country, were now face-to-face with local communities over simmering disputes arising out of the new land investment deals they had signed with the Koroma government. An Oakland Institute report, released in June 2011, stated that there was a tremendous lack of transparency and disclosure over land investment deals and mining agreements signed between government officials and the new multinationals that arrived in Sierra Leone after Koroma assumed power. Towards mid-2012, when African Minerals and London Mining intensified their iron ore operations, government officials in Freetown boasted that Sierra Leone's economy was one of the fastest growing in the world. But these claims of economic growth were only temporal and largely based on speculated revenue inflows anticipated from the many shady deals and concessionary agreements signed between Koroma and the flood of international corporations that occupied strategic economic interests in the country. In reality, however, the anticipated growth essentially meant that London Mining, African Minerals, Vimetco, Bollore Africa Logistics, Addax Bioenergy, Socfin International, African Petroleum, and Chevron, among others, became the new economic giants driving foreign capital investments and economic activities in Sierra Leone. They paid little dividends and enjoyed tremendous tax breaks from mineral exports while local patrons (the national political elites) stuffed the meager financial royalty payments into their private bank accounts in Europe's offshore tax heavens.

The numerous multinational corporate influx that followed Koroma's neo-liberal agenda was anchored on a sloppy chart: despite its avowed claims of economic growth and development, global development indexes ranked the country among the most repressive economies in the world. In 2013, a year before the Ebola outbreak, the International Monetary Fund (IMF) stated that more than half of Sierra Leone's six million people (mostly unemployed urban youths) lived on less than a dollar a day in the teeming slums of Freetown. Political repression, state corruption, and graft that accompanied Koroma's ascension to power were reawakening the ghosts of dictatorship, national theft, and underdevelopment of the pre-war years. The new foundation of good governance whose roots germinated after the civil war was now plagued by rank opportunism, political sycophancy, and an emerging *tribo-regional* cronyism of Koroma's political circle. The pervasive state corruption, incestuous corporatization and institutionalized deification of the presidency, which became hallmarks of Koroma's corporatist agenda, meant that the post-war national democratic character, built out of the ashes of the war, assumed a path towards authoritarianism.

A Transparency International report in 2014, the year of the Ebola outbreak, ranked Sierra Leone 119 out of 175 countries for corruption. A previous Transparency International corruption survey released a year earlier confirmed that ninety percent of Sierra Leoneans confessed to having bribed police and/or judicial officials for issues ranging from unwarranted traffic tickets to evading false arrest and to paying government officials for administrative services. Sierra Leone's corruption ratings ironically became increasingly alarming since 2008, the year when additional anti-corruption legislations were introduced. Under Koroma, theft of public resources extended from kickbacks on awarded state construction projects to pilferage from donor-funded development assistance budgets. An audit of a US$13.2 million United States Agency for International Development (USAID) fund for food and agricultural development in Sierra Leone conducted in December 2011, discovered unreasonable expenses of US$794,664 by the government of Sierra Leone which could not be verified. A year later in 2012, the inundating corruption within the health ministry of Sierra Leone caused the GAVI Alliance to halt a US$5 million anti-malaria campaign due to misuse of donor funds. It was within this environment of authoritarian democracy, of state corruption and of incestuous corporate investments that the 2014 Ebola outbreak unfolded.

When initial reports of unprecedented deaths first emerged in the eastern district of Kailahun, government officials in Freetown denied the outbreak in the country. They felt Freetown was a safe distance from the initial site of the outbreak (Kailahun is a distance of over 300 kilometers from Freetown). Political elites in Freetown never treated the unfolding epidemic with seriousness. The outbreak appeared within the same geographical space where, in March 1991, an armed insurgency started and spread to every village, town, and district across the country, leaving behind unprecedented numbers of casualties and deaths. Back in 1991, government officials in Freetown adopted a dismissive attitude towards the start of a rebellion that later overwhelmed the entire country and tore it apart for a decade, eventually warranting the deployment of massive foreign armies and troops of aid organizations. As the Ebola death toll swelled in Kailahun, journalists in Freetown quoted a government minister as attributing the death reports to opposition propaganda designed to undermine support for the government. The government's lack of a response translated into state denial of the outbreak, while local journalists and civil society activists mounted a sustained campaign of pressure calling for an all-out national response to stop the outbreak. Newspapers decried the government's inaction; it appeared the outbreak was not a priority on the national agenda.

The Sierra Leone National Response to the Outbreak

What was responsible for the non-prioritization of the national response to the outbreak? Did the outbreak take the government of Sierra Leone by surprise in any way? And did the national emergency laws eventually invoked in response to the outbreak actually help to stem the rising tide of infections and death? These questions are at the core of the national response of the government of Sierra Leone to the outbreak. The answers to these questions address why the extremely robust military measures invoked by the Sierra Leone government did very little to contain the outbreak.

It should be remembered that, at the time of the outbreak, the operations of leading government functionaries in Freetown were largely anchored on Koroma's political party consolidation plans. In fact, a national convention of his party, All Peoples Congress (APC), held in 2013 endorsed Koroma for the third time as chairman and leader of the party immediately. This was a few months after the controversial presidential elections of 2012 that gave him a second presidential term. During the convention Koroma threatened potential successors with severe consequences, all in a bid to suppress internal party opposition and dissent. National party executive positions, including that of the party leadership for which Koroma was endorsed, were never contested or challenged. Koroma's staunch loyal supporters staffed all national positions of the party, including the deputy leadership position. Potential contenders to Koroma's leadership position within the party, including his vice president, were marginalized from participation at the convention.

After the convention, Koroma focused his attention on a new political agenda in the country; his supporters started a campaign for a constitutional amendment to allow Koroma a third-term in office. Leonard Balogun Koroma, his 2012 elections campaign coordinator who would later be appointed transport minister, and another party spokesperson, Robin Fallay, started mobilizations in support of a third term agenda for Koroma. At the time of the outbreak, when deaths and infections were constantly reported in eastern Sierra Leone, Koroma and his supporters were largely focused on the third term campaign in Freetown. On April 27, 2014, during a road opening ceremony along the hillside of Freetown on the Jui-Regent highway, Koroma assured those promoting his third term agenda that they were exercising their rights to free speech. Before the ceremony, tens of thousands of t-shirts were distributed to Koroma's supporters. Monies, amounting to millions of taxpayers' funds, were spent on the mobilizations for the ceremony. As Koroma's political celebrations continued in Freetown and his supporters plotted his third-term roadmap, the outbreak was sporadically claiming many lives in the eastern districts of Sierra Leone.

By this time, the Ebola Management Center in Kenema alone had lost twenty-eight health workers, including two doctors, nurses, lab technicians, and some ambulance drivers. In some of the referral hospitals across the country, health workers had gone on strikes over non-payment of allowances and lack of basic personal protective equipment. Many hospitals had no gloves, stretchers, and other isolation supplies needed by nurses and doctors caring for Ebola patients. Barely a month after Koroma's political celebrations at the Jui-Regent road-opening ceremony, the outbreak became a full-blown national nightmare; the infections and deaths spread to most parts of the country. The government's inaction and failure to rapidly respond to the unfolding catastrophe when it first began ultimately resulted in irreparable damages: countless deaths and infections were hitting every community in the country.

Frustrated by this unfolding situation and the inaction of senior government officials, the business and mining community threatened to withdraw its essential staff from Sierra Leone in early July if drastic steps to stop Ebola were not taken. By then, the eastern districts were in dire conditions and protests by health care workers had even erupted in Kenema. With the threat of expatriate business workers pulling out of the country, Koroma announced on July 18, 2015, that the government had created an Emergency Operations Center (EOC) to deal with the unfolding catastrophe. But the Koroma government's response still remained slow until the death of the country's leading Ebola doctor, 39-year-old Sheikh Umar Khan. The outbreak was never clearly prioritized by the Koroma administration from the very start. Subsequent measures assumed by Koroma in the following months after Khan's death were mainly spontaneous and largely population containment actions aimed at suppressing the rising dissent and anger that resulted from the government's slow and ineffective response to the outbreak.

After Khan died, for instance, Koroma declared a public health emergency in the country, assuming strategic draconian measures that included new executive orders which empowered the police and army to support health workers in identifying and containing the chain of transmission. Around this time, the horrific accounts of the rising deaths and infections figures, now headline news in the local and international press, resulted in serious blame on Koroma. People calling into radio talk shows blamed the widespread explosion of the outbreak on the president's failure to seriously deal with the virus when it first began. It took the president five weeks to issue an official statement on the epidemic. He never visited any of the areas affected by the disease until ten weeks into the outbreak, and only did so after persistent pressure from the local press and a section of civil society.

On August 15, 2014, when Koroma issued his first public statement on the crisis, he tried to avoid responsibility for the outbreak. He blamed the international community for the country's failure to confront the Ebola virus. "I am disappointed at the international community in their delay in responding towards the fight against the deadly Ebola virus in Sierra Leone. We have not been provided with enough equipment, resources, qualified health officers, and we have lost the only expert we had in the country to the disease amidst the declaration of the international health emergency on Ebola," Koroma said in a press release issued by the State House Communications Unit.

The government shifted away its responsibility to handle its own affairs. Koroma's blame on the international community for the deteriorating situation was indicative of government's inability and unwillingness to deal with the emergency. Report of the outbreak in West Africa was announced months earlier, but the Sierra Leone government failed to adequately prepare for the unfolding catastrophe regardless of local pressure and appeals. The Association of Nurses and Sierra Leone Medical and Dental Association were never engaged by authorities to discuss the situation during the initial stages of the outbreak. When the outbreak was announced in the country, Sierra Leone's health ministry was totally unprepared. Health workers in Sierra Leone reported, at the early days of the outbreak, that the stockpiled Ebola test kits had already expired and that the personal protective equipment (PPEs) used by the health workers were totally inadequate for the Ebola response efforts. Even before Sheikh Umar Khan's death, several frontline health workers had been infected and many died due to a lack of basic protective gears and equipment, necessities such as facemasks, stretchers, mattresses, protective gloves, and other isolation supplies.

A foreign diplomat told the *New York Times* in October 2014 that Koroma's emergency response was a complete mess. The diplomat said no one appeared to be in charge of the Emergency Operations Center (EOC), the Sierra Leone government's agency established in response to the crisis by Koroma. "Different factions made decisions independently," the diplomat told the *New York Times*. Indeed, the EOC, established supposedly as an emergency office to coordinate the efforts of national and international groups involved in the response efforts, operated out of the WHO local office in Freetown, but technically it was still under the management of Sierra Leone's health ministry. The health ministry itself had been inundated with some of the scariest corruption and graft scandals since Koroma assumed power. A year before the outbreak, twenty-nine of the ministry's top health officials were indicted in relation to the theft of over half-million dollars in donor funds allocated for a vaccination program. All indicted persons were later freed following a court trial that found them not guilty of the corruption charges. A free health care program set up by foreign donors was also damaged by similar corruption scandals. A former health minister was convicted in 2010 on corruption charges. At the time of the outbreak, the corruption reputation of Sierra Leone's health ministry had reached alarming heights across global health circles. Nearly all so-called donor funded health initiatives of Koroma's administration had suffered tremendous setbacks or collapsed due to administrative mismanagement, graft and inefficiency. In the wake of the outbreak, questions emerged regarding the competency of Koroma's choice of a health minister.

The health minister, Miatta Kargbo, had no experience in medicine and was already at odds with Sierra Leone's medical community even before the outbreak. In 2013, she condemned doctors who had gone on strike over unpaid salaries as greedy. When the outbreak was reported in Sierra Leone, Kargbo appeared before parliament on June 17, 2015, and blamed Ebola victims in Kailahun for their own infections. Kargbo said a female nurse had brought the illness upon herself because she slept with a boyfriend who was infected. "They stayed in the same house and throughout the process when he was infected, they were sleeping together in the same room as boyfriend and girlfriend," she told parliamentarians.

Kargbo's incompetent leadership over the health ministry added to the general confusion that resulted from Koroma's spontaneous handling of the crisis. Even within the cabinet there were dissensions regarding Kargbo's capacity to deal with the workload of the health ministry and the rising pressure exerted on its officials by the exploding outbreak. Kargbo's colleagues complained of her arrogance and disdain for other officials within government. Some wondered why Koroma continuously retained her as health minister regardless of the public outcry and condemnation of her leadership of the ministry. Incompetence within the health ministry, massive public corruption, the lack of an effectively coordinated national response, and absence of the outbreak's genuine prioritization all translated into an organized state confusion. The outbreak found a fertile terrain amidst this context and thrived in its onslaught, claiming more deaths, more infections, and additional geographical space. The casualties of the outbreak overwhelmed the national response, disorganized and confused as it was.

In the middle of this ensuing confusion, Koroma adopted additional robust measures. He was now forced to act by the rapidly deteriorating situation. Around this time, in early August 2014, the United States government considered the outbreak in Freetown a serious cause for concern and mandated its embassy to evacuate family members of embassy staff and personnel. The numbers of infected people had tripled and the death numbers had similarly climbed in the four months since emergency laws were imposed. The robust measures – quarantines, lockdowns, travel restrictions, and checkpoints – only increased people's suffering and added to the general chaos in the national response.

International aid workers and CDC officials deployed in West Africa spoke of security concerns and the potential risks of full-scale violence erupting in the region in protests against national response mechanisms. Reports of isolated protests and attacks against health workers and ambulance drivers across the country were featured in local media coverage. This boiling state of potential instability ushered in a draconian climate, resulting principally from Koroma's handling of the crisis; he now saw the epidemic with military eyes and assumed robust military powers in his response to the raging public health crisis and its potential instability.

Koroma eventually fired health minister Miatta Kargbo the same week the United States issued a mandate to withdraw its non-essential staff from Freetown. Abu Bakarr Fofanah, Kargbo's former deputy, was named the new minister of health, and Madina Rahman, a Koroma operative, was also appointed his deputy. At the same time, Stephen Gaojia, a former minister, was appointed head of the EOC to head the national Ebola response. Gaojia declared a three-day national lockdown and house-to-house search operations, a move initially claimed to be a success but later declared a sham and wastage of resources. The EOC had been riddled by failure due to inefficient strategy and a daunting bureaucratic arrangement crowded by national officials and international aid staff. Koroma eventually dismantled the EOC, created a National Ebola Response Center (NERC), appointed defense minister Palo Conteh as its head, and turned the Ebola response efforts over to the Sierra Leone military. Then on November 5, 2015, Koroma caused parliament to validate his assumption of section 29 of the Sierra Leone Constitution, under which he was empowered to arrest and detain any individual without a court order or formal indictment as part of his emergency laws. By this time, the British and Chinese armies were already in the country carrying out their diverse response agendas.

Ebola as Pretext to Suppress Opponents and Dissent

Koroma's new regulations did not only change the Ebola response plan and its staff, but it gave birth to a new political climate: corruption stories, arrests of journalists, and suppression of dissent followed the militarization of the country with the introduction of additional robust measures. The ugly stories of suppression, of individual sufferings, of police brutality, and of the selective application of emergency laws appeared as frontline news in daily press coverage of the outbreak. Only a few weeks after Paolo Conteh took charge of the NERC, radio journalist David Tam-Baryoh was arrested after he hosted an opposition politician on a radio talk show that listed a chain of abusive applications of Ebola control measures. During the radio show, Tam-Baryoh and his guest the opposition politician questioned the effectiveness of the national Ebola response and cited instances of mismanagement of Ebola funds. Tam-Baryoh was later arrested by a presidential order and detained for eleven days without a charge under the emergency laws.

Opposition political party members and supporters accused Koroma of using emergency laws and the outbreak to crackdown on free speech and democratic rights. Some said he was using the Ebola epidemic and state of emergency to "create a police state in Sierra Leone." A month after Tam-Baryoh's arrest, several protests erupted in Kono district following tensions between police and supporters of ousted vice president Samuel Sam Sumana. Scores of youths, including a sister of the vice president, were randomly arrested on allegations of having threatened violence and violating emergency laws.[138] It later appeared that Koroma directly ordered the targeted and selective arrests under the emergency laws. Additionally, two women and six men from Kono were arrested and ordered detained for six months without charge by Koroma over an alleged dispute relating to a contested Ebola suspect. Another group of five youths were also arbitrarily arrested under the same presidential orders between February and March 2015. Independent enquiries later revealed that the arrested individuals were detained because they supported the vice president, who Koroma was determined to remove from the ruling party.[139]

As police continued the use of emergency laws to crackdown on youth protests in Kono, it became clear that Koroma was using the outbreak's response measures and laws to brutally settle internal party dissent towards his leadership and also muzzle external political opposition to his style of governance. An *Africa Confidential* article published in June 2015 stated that Koroma's removal of Samuel Sam-Sumana from the vice presidency position was based on Koroma's fears that Sam-Sumana was building support for a bid to succeed him as president. "Koroma was alarmed because his deputy was courting important factions of the governing All People's Congress (APC) and building up momentum," the *Africa Confidential* article stated.[140]

The deliberate use of the outbreak for corrupt accumulation, embezzlement of donor funds, and abuse of constitutional authority hindered the real fight against the outbreak. Towards the end of 2014 when police brutality intensified in Kono, the WHO announced an alarming discovery in the district: eighty-seven bodies were found buried and a hundred and nineteen cases of infections were officially reported in Kono during the first ten days of December 2014. This was around the same time police amplified brutal actions against protesting youths, mainly supporters of the vice president, Sam-Sumana, whose long-drawn out political struggle with Koroma and his henchmen in government was at its tipping point.

By the time Koroma unceremoniously led the expulsion of Sam-Sumana from the ruling party and dismissed him from the vice presidency, his wrongful use of the state of emergency laws to suppress opponents and frustrate democratic rights had reached its peak. Local and international human rights groups then realized that an alarming climate of repression was resulting from government's

---

[138] Henry Tamba, "VP's Sister, APC Youth Chairman and Others Arrested In Kono" by Komba-Kpakoi, Voice of Binkongoh, October 27, 2015 (www.voice-of-binkongoh.info/vps-sister-apc-youth-chairman-and-others-arrested-in-kono).

[139] Alusine Sesay, "CARL & AdvocAid concerned over 'arbitrary' arrest and detention of Kono Youths," *Concord Times*, April 22, 2015 (slconcordtimes.com/carl-advocaid-concerned-over-arbitrary-arrest-and-detention-of-kono-youths).

[140] "Sierra Leone: The Discord Lingers On," *Africa Confidential* 56, No. 13, 26 June 2015 (www.africa-confidential.com).

handling of the outbreak. National and international groups expressed immediate concerns over the deteriorating human rights violations and abuse of democratic principles in the country. The Sierra Leone Human Rights Commission on April 23, 2015, for example, issued a press release and condemned Koroma's discriminatory implementation of the emergency laws. The Commission said it was worried that pro-Koroma groups were allowed to hold meetings and voice opinions on national questions while other groups considered anti-government were repeatedly denied the same opportunity to meet and discuss issues affecting the country. The Commission's statement came after police disrupted a meeting of the Sierra Leone Bar Association held at the Law Courts building in Freetown to discuss the constitutional merits of Koroma's dismissal of the vice president. Police alleged that the meeting violated the emergency laws. The week preceding the Commission's statement another group of opposition party members were arrested by police in Freetown for organizing a peaceful protest at the gates of the United States Embassy. They were arrested three days after they protested against the president's wrongful use of emergency laws against his opponents. Four days following the Commission's statement, police proceeded and also used the emergency laws to ban a planned march by the Sierra Leone Association of Journalists (SLAJ) to launch a women's leadership campaign against Ebola. Police similarly alleged that anti-government operatives planned on using the proposed peaceful march to protest against non-Ebola matters.[141]

The ongoing list of human rights violations and anti-democratic actions of the government forced Amnesty International to join the Sierra Leone Human Rights Commission in condemning the government's wrongful use of emergency laws. Sabrina Mahtani, Amnesty International's West Africa researcher, called on the Sierra Leone government to stop the use of the emergency regulations brought in to combat Ebola as a prefoottext to restrict freedom of expression and peaceful assembly.[142] The organization was concerned that a senior regional human rights officer and fifteen other opposition party members were arrested following a protest at the regional office of the Sierra Leone People's Party (SLPP) in Kenema. Police claimed that those arrested violated the emergency laws. Reportedly, the arrested human rights officer had recently criticized the police on a radio station for the wrongful use of emergency laws to violate civil liberties and individual freedoms.

The government continued its brutal response to citizen's protests despite these growing concerns and criticisms from local and international organizations.

---

[141] Ibrahim Tarawalie, "HRC frowns at 'bias implementation of Emergency Regulations". *Concord Times*, April 24, 2015 (slconcordtimes.com/hrc-frowns-at-bias-implementation-of-emergency-regulations).

[142] See, for additional information, Amnesty International's Press Release, "Sierra Leone: Ebola Regulations and Other Laws must not be used to curtail Freedom of Expression and Assembly," May 4, 2015 (www.amnesty.org/en/latest/news/2015/05/sierra-leone-ebola-regulations-and-other-laws-must-not-be-used-to-curtail-freedom-of-expression-and-assembly).

On one occasion, a man named Ansumana Bangura was given a six-month prison sentence for allegedly insulting the president in front of a police officer. And another, Mahmoud Tim Kargbo, was also detained for several months and charged with five counts of defamatory libel for forwarding a social media message critical of the president's actions even though he did not write the message.[143]

These grave injustices and violations continued in the full glare of the thousands of international aid workers and hundreds of representatives of international governments who constantly visited the country, yet these international representatives failed to raise the issues when they met Koroma to discuss the outbreak. The United States and its European allies, for example, closed their eyes on the numerous cases of human rights violations and public theft commissioned by Koroma and his government. In fact, the international community, led by the United States, intensified support for Koroma and his presidential colleagues regardless of the persistent complaint and demonstrations that were staged around the world against the excesses and violations of the Sierra Leone government. The April 2015 youth demonstrations in front of the United States embassy in Freetown, in particular, were a direct response to Obama's public endorsement of the corruption and human rights violations of Koroma. The action of the youths in Freetown was a calculated strategy to send a direct message to Washington that Obama's praise of Koroma was not reflective of the corrupt and undemocratic leadership of the three West African presidents. The youths knew that State Department officials, in particular, were aware that a constitutional crisis was created in Sierra Leone by Koroma's unconstitutional dismissal of the vice president just a few weeks before his Washington trip. They were aware that a national audit report in Sierra Leone confirmed that public officials in Koroma's government stole funds donated to the Ebola fight.

State Department officials were fully in possession of relevant information relating to the corruption of Koroma's administration. A 2013 diplomatic notice sent by United States embassy staff in Freetown revealed that Koroma held a ten percent personal-share in Addax Bioenergy, the Swiss ethanol company that has millions of dollars in a sprawling sugar plantation in the northern district of Bombali (the home of Koroma). An audit report on missing Ebola funds implicated individuals and companies tied directly to Koroma's business associates. In June 2015, *Africa Confidential* reported that a US$1.1 million contract for the purchase of 20 ambulances was awarded to a fictitious Lebanese company owned by Koroma's squash-playing friend, Mahmoud Bahsoon. It alleged that Koroma offered the contract to Bahsoon on a squash pitch while the two were playing a game. "The president telephoned the then minister of health, Miatta Kargbo, to

---

[143] Amara, Hawa S, "Defamatory Libel Against President Koroma Takes One To Prison," *The New Storm*, March 20, 2015 (www.newstormsl.com/index.php/other-news/135-defamatory-libel-against-president-koroma-takes-one-to-prison).

arrange for an advance payment of 50% of the contract to Bahsoon on the following day. The money was disbursed even before the contract documents were put together," the *Africa Confidential* stated.[144]

Representatives of western governments knew these stories of corruption stemmed from the top echelons of the Sierra Leone government, but they did not speak about them. They knew that the Ebola response efforts were hampered by the misappropriation of the funds donated to the fight against the outbreak. They were aware that Koroma saw the outbreak as an opportunity to consolidate his grip on power and used the health crisis and the emergency laws to suppress opposition, undermine democratic values, contain free speech, and violate individual freedoms. The United States government, in particular, took the lead in endorsing and supporting the undemocratic practices and authoritarian tendencies of Koroma and the pervasive corruption of his appointed officials. Whenever Koroma's opponents raised questions relating to abuse of national democratic rights, they were challenged by Koroma's propagandists with the public statements of western leaders and governments that endorsed Koroma as a democratic leader. These deliberate actions of western governments in support of Koroma and his corrupt officials not only undermined the fight against the outbreak, but also helped to fuel the monstrous character of a vicious authoritarian democracy that has evolved into a full-blown despotic regime with no regard for constitution and the rule of law. Koroma's declaration of state of emergency laws was not genuinely aimed at halting the casualties of the outbreak. Rather, it was a political decision in pursuit of his political ambition. His continued retention of the emergency laws and ongoing ban on public gatherings are part of his plans to keep both the internal opposition within his party and the external opposition tamed, via draconian military and police power. Sadly, this had been accomplished with the active support and endorsement of western governments, including the United States.

---

[144] 'Sierra Leone: The Discord Lingers On,' *Africa Confidential* 56, No, 13, 26 June 2015 (www.africa-confidential.com).

PART THREE
SOCIO-CULTURAL AND
ECONOMIC IMPACTS OF EBOLA

CHAPTER 7

THE SOCIO-CULTURAL IMPACTS OF THE EBOLA OUTBREAK

> *Most of the patients are in undemocratic countries with very corrupt systems. If they complain, they are threatened. They are told their children will receive no more medicines from America and their men will go to prison. The issue is the world's poorest communities are used as guinea pigs by the world's richest, and legitimate scientific debate of these issues is stifled by corporate intimidation...*
> — John Le Carre, *The Constant Gardener*[145]

In December 2014, the Pulitzer Prize winning science writer and senior fellow for global health at the Council on Foreign Relations, Laurie Garrett, wrote that the most intense Ebola epidemic in the world was to be found in Sierra Leone.[146] Garrett's article, which appeared in the *Foreign Policy Magazine* on December 11, 2014, was published at a time when the outbreak in Sierra Leone had reached its most alarming point. The country had witnessed more than five hundred new laboratory-confirmed cases per week.[147] Worst still, there were hundreds more suspected infections that were unaccounted for in the daily reports. Two months before this, on October 1, 2014, Save the Children (a British charity) warned of a terrifying situation: the number of new cases was doubling every few weeks.

"At the current rate, ten people every hour will be infected with Ebola in the

---

[145] *The Constant Gardener* (2005), directed by Fernando Meirelles, with Ralph Fiennes as Justin Quayle, set in the slums in Kibera and Loiyangalani, Kenya; the poverty so affected the film crew that they established the Constant Gardener Trust to provide basic education to those areas (John le Carré is a patron of the charity).

[146] Laurie Garrett, "Facing Death Without Spreading Disease. Foreign Policy," December 11, 2014 (foreignpolicy.com/2014/12/11/facing-death-without-spreading-disease-ebola-sierra-leone), Web. 1 Aug. 2015.

[147] WHO's Ebola Situation Report released on November 26, 2014 stated that the total number of Ebola cases reported in Sierra Leone since the outbreak began was eclipsing the number reported from Liberia and Guinea.

country before the end of October," Save the Children reported.[148]

Like the hundreds of western reporters and foreign correspondents who flooded the region, Garrett travelled to West Africa two months after Save the Children issued its alarm on the deteriorating situation in Sierra Leone. To understand the main cause of this terrifying situation, Garrett claimed that the widespread explosion of the outbreak in Sierra Leone was due to West African cultural factors, specifically centuries old traditional burial practices, including the washing of the dead.

"Stopping the nation's epidemic means all burials must be safe ones, and all ailing Ebola sufferers must be removed from the care of loved ones and placed in humane, isolated treatment facilities," she argued in one of the three major dispatches she wrote on her trip to the region.[149]

Garrett, one of western media's best science reporters, was actually dictating a western script based on an outbreak narrative developed by western scientists and popularized by leading news organizations in Europe and America. It is a narrative that blamed the origin and massive widespread transmission of the outbreak on African cultural behavior and supposed abuse of African environmental habitats. To justify this position, Garrett used the story of a 38-year-old woman named Musu Esther Massaquoi, a resident of Freetown who was jailed by a Freetown judge for allegedly obstructing an Ebola burial team (a group of young men dressed in moon suits and escorted by armed police officers) from performing its functions. Musu Massaquoi's story appeared in a local newspaper in Freetown a few months before the arrival of Garrett in Sierra Leone.[150] The local newspaper reported the story of how a magistrate court in Freetown convicted and sentenced Massaquoi to a year imprisonment or an alternative fine of five hundred thousand Leones (the equivalent of US$115) for having allegedly obstructed an Ebola burial team from taking away the corpse of an Ebola victim. The said Ebola victim was Massaquoi's sister who was infected in late October. Musu Massaquoi reportedly called the Ebola emergency hotline to send an ambulance team to transport her sister to a treatment center. The ambulance team never showed up, and a few days later, her sister died at home, attended to by Massaquoi. After her death, Musu Massaquoi and other family members prepared the body for a traditional funeral; which involves selected adults washing the body and wrapping the entire body in white clothed linens before burial. But a government burial team accompanied by armed police officers arrived at the Massaquoi's

---

[148] Save the Children report, "Desperate demand for Ebola treatment in Sierra Leone as five people are infected every hour." - See more at: www.savethechildren.org.uk/2014-10/desperate-demand-ebola-treatment-sierra-leone-5-people-are-infected-every-hour-0#sthash.fUXRoLdI.dpuf.

[149] Laurie Garrett, "Facing Death Without Spreading Disease. Foreign Policy," December 11, 2014 (foreignpolicy.com/2014/12/11/facing-death-without-spreading-disease-ebola-sierra-leone), Web. 1 Aug. 2015.

[150] Aminata Phidelia Allie, "Woman convicted for Obstructing Ebola Teams," *Politico Newspaper*, November 07, 2014 (politicosl.com/2014/11/woman-convicted-for-obstructing-ebola-teams), Web. July 2015.

home; they stopped the funeral, took away the corpse and eventually arrested Musu Massaquoi.

A few days later, she was charged with three counts of violating the public emergency regulations, the national legislation passed by Ernest Koroma in July 2014 in response to the outbreak. Under the new emergency regulations, the president ordered the arrest and detention of potential Ebola patients and any family members who harbored the sick and the deceased.

Disease Conflation Strategy: The Outbreak's Transmission Agency

Since July 2014 when national emergency laws were declared by the president, the military and police erected roadblocks and checkpoints to screen vehicles and travelers for signs and symptoms consistent with the Ebola virus. These signs and symptoms were not rare nor specific to Ebola: they included fever, diarrhea, vomiting, red eyes, body rash, persistent severe headaches, abdominal pain, bleeding, fatigue, muscular pain and other similar symptoms.[151] These are the same signs and symptoms of endemic diseases in the rain forest belt of the Mano River countries of West Africa: malaria, yellow fever, typhoid, measles, chicken pox, small pox, and Lassa fever.

In Sierra Leone, the statistics for malaria have remained at all-time highs over the last three decades. The 2013 malaria indicator survey conducted by Statistics Sierra Leone – a year before the Ebola outbreak – acknowledged the stable and perennial enmity of malaria transmission in the country. "Malaria is endemic in Sierra Leone with stable and perennial transmission in all parts of the country," the report stated, adding that the entire population remained at risk of developing the disease. "Malaria accounts for about fifty percent of outpatient morbidity and is presently the leading cause of morbidity and mortality among children under age five," the report stated.[152] Health Ministry reports in 2013 estimated that child mortality in Sierra Leone attributed to malaria was around thirty-eight percent for children below five years and twenty-five percent for all other ages of the population. The report also noted that thirty-three percent of children under five years had reported fevers, and that Kailahun, which became the epicenter of the Ebola outbreak in 2014, recorded the highest percentage of children with fever in 2013.[153] The WHO World Malaria Report of 2012 reported an estimated 219 million cases of malaria worldwide, and 660,000 malaria deaths globally in 2010 with eighty percent of the cases and ninety percent of deaths reportedly occurring in

---

[151] List of signs and symptoms of Ebola hemorrhagic fever issued by the United States Centers for Disease Control (CDC). See: www.cdc.gov/vhf/ebola/symptoms.

[152] Outpatient morbidity statistics, MoHS, 2009, MIS 2010, Malaria Indicator Survey 2013 Report, National Malaria Control Program, Statistics Sierra Leone February 2013.

[153] Sierra Leone Malaria Indicator Survey (2013). National Malaria Control Program: Statistic Sierra Leone and Ministry of Health and Sanitation, Freetown, February 2013. Pp. 41-43.

Africa, where children under five years of age and pregnant women accounted for the largest portion of the statistic.[154]

Additionally, in 2012 Sierra Leone recorded 22,885 cases of diarrhea and 298 deaths due to cholera. The UN Office for the Co-ordination of Humanitarian Affairs (OCHA) said the 2012 cholera outbreak in Sierra Leone was the worst in fifteen years; ten of the country's thirteen districts were severely affected. Around the same time, Guinea reported a massive cholera outbreak in nine of the country's thirty-three districts. OCHA confirmed at the time that the capital, Conakry, had 3,247 cases alone by February 2012. The outbreak in Guinea was linked to the situation in Sierra Leone.[155]

"We have seen a dramatic increase in the last five to six weeks in cases, especially in Freetown," Amanda McClelland, the Africa emergency health adviser at the International Federation of Red Cross and Red Crescent Societies (IFRC) told the UK *Guardian* on September 5, 2012.[156] "The conditions in Freetown are the perfect storm for cholera. We know we haven't contained it by any means, and it has the potential of increasing further and becoming a regional issue," she added.

A month earlier on August 7, 2012, the president of Sierra Leone Ernest Koroma had declared the outbreak a national public health crisis. Aid organizations came to the rescue: a national treatment program was ramped up in response to the outbreak.

"Our present cholera treatment facilities are stretched to the limit with patients. Everybody is at risk," Karen Van den Brande, then head of the *Médecins Sans Frontières* (MSF) mission in Sierra Leone said.[157] Political leaders in Sierra Leone and staff of international aid organizations attributed the cholera outbreak to the lack of access to safe drinking water. Sierra Leone's then deputy energy and water resources minister, Martin Bash Kamara, acknowledged that the pipe water system in Freetown contributed to the cholera infections. "There are many broken water pipes flowing with water which need to be fixed in many parts of the city," he admitted. UNICEF officials in Sierra Leone also agreed that lack of clean drinking water was the underlying cause for cholera outbreaks in West Africa.

Indeed, records of international aid organizations put the countries of the Mano River region of West Africa within the world's lowest ratings for access to water and sanitation. In Sierra Leone, UNICEF reported in 2012 that only 12.8%

---

[154] World Health Organization (WHO) World Malaria Report 2012 (www.who.int/malaria/publications/world_malaria_report_2012/en/index.html).

[155] WHO Global Task Force on Cholera Control: Cholera Country Profile Report for Sierra Leone, January 22, 2013. See: www.who.int/cholera/countries/SierraLeoneCountryProfile2013.pdf.

[156] "Cholera sweeps across Sierra Leone and Guinea Following Severe Rainfall," *The Guardian*, September 5, 2012 (www.theguardian.com/global-development/2012/sep/05/cholera-sierra-leone-guinea-severe-rainfall), 30 July 2015.

[157] For additional information see: www.theguardian.com/global-development/2012/sep/05/cholera-sierra-leone-guinea-severe-rainfall

of Sierra Leone's six million people had access to proper sanitation, and 42.9% had no access to clean drinking water. The same UNICEF report stated that only 19% of the Guinean population had access to improved sanitation, and half the country's ten million people had access to safe drinking water sources.[158] These horrible health statistics meant that the communities of the rain forest belt of the Mano River region were highly disease prone and they continually recorded endemic statistics of deaths and illness that are directly associated with water-borne or water-related diseases: deaths and diseases linked to cholera, malaria, typhoid fevers, dysentery, Lassa fever, and other rickettsia (germ and bacterial) infections are replete in the reports of national agencies and aid groups in the region. In 2014, all of the signs and symptoms associated with these age-old endemic rickettsia infections were included into the long list of signs and symptoms associated with the Ebola virus.

The conflation of the signs and symptoms of all these rickettsia diseases by national authorities into the Ebola response efforts intensified the pressure on the dilapidated health systems of the Mano River countries and ultimately confounded the effectiveness of the national response to the outbreak. In Sierra Leone, for example, this disease-conflated approach to epidemiological response did not just confound the national response mechanism, but it may have accelerated the speed and agency of disease transmission and casualties during the outbreak. The militarization of the country, the criminalization of private medical practice and proscription of illness all meant that the poorly equipped public facilities, relying predominantly on non-conventional methods of diagnosis, became unnecessarily crowded and eventually plunged into operational chaos: lack of equipment, insufficient personnel and inadequate knowledge of disease epidemiology among local doctors placed both health workers and patients suffering from usual rickettsia diseases at risks of infection and death. In November 2014, when Sierra Leone led the charts on Ebola infections and deaths, aid groups expressed concerns that the devotion of entire health services to the Ebola response affected treatment and care for other known health conditions. Government's handling of every sick person as a potential Ebola patient affected pregnant women and babies in need of health care. Families of pregnant women who visited PCMH Children's Hospital in Freetown gave chilling accounts of how midwives abandoned women in labor for fear of contracting the Ebola virus. Patients' refusal to visit hospitals and treatment centers were predominately driven by the lack of properly secured containment measures at public hospitals across Sierra Leone. Most individuals reportedly absconded from public hospitals due to perceived fears that hospitals were potential infectious zones: they mixed both potential Ebola patients and

---

[158] UNICEF statistics quoted by the UK *Guardian* in its report on the 2012 cholera outbreaks in Sierra Leone and Guinea. See for additional information: www.savethechildren.org.uk/2014-10/desperate-demand-ebola-treatment-sierra-leone-5-people-are-infected-every-hour-0#sthash.fUXRoLdI.dpuf

non-Ebola patients.

On December 10, 2014, for example, Laurie Garrett reported a telling experience on the quagmire of the Connaught Hospital in Freetown during the Ebola outbreak. "It was a terribly disturbing sight. Connaught Hospital in central Freetown looked unremarkable," Garrett wrote in the *Foreign Policy Magazine*. At the time of Garrett's report, Connaught Hospital, which operated an eighteen bed Ebola unit, was heavily flooded with patients who were mostly left in the open air of the hospital's entrance.

"These men lying in the street without toilet facilities, food, or water could not get into hospital beds until they were vacated. The less fortunate die in the isolation ward, or out on the street inside the pen, waiting for space to free up. Turnaround time on lab work averages three to four days in Sierra Leone; so most patients die here, without ever learning whether or not it is the Ebola virus that is driving their fever, diarrhea, vomiting, and hemorrhaging," Garrett observed.[159] While Garrett's observation may have been predicated on the notion of herculean challenges faced by international aid workers on the ground (at the time Connaught Hospital's Ebola program was managed by British aid workers mainly from the London-based King's Health Partners), the central issue was how the government's conflated approach to the outbreak plunged the entire health service of Sierra Leone into tremendous crisis. It is within the confines of the militarized national response, which conflated all the usual endemic disease symptoms into the Ebola outbreak and simultaneously criminalized and proscribed private medical practice and illness, that the widespread explosion of the virus and its massive death numbers can be located and attributed.

Western Journalists and Demonization of African Culture

The dilapidated health infrastructures of the Mano River countries relied principally on non-laboratory diagnostic methods for disease identification and treatment, and when confronted with conflated national response strategies they could not adequately and efficiently handle all of the emerging health demands and challenges of an epidemiological crisis. Therefore, the reports of western journalists, which regarded African behavioral patterns – traditional funeral rites and care for the sick – as the cause of widespread infections could not sufficiently explain the actual agency of transmission during the outbreak. The proscription of traditional funerals by national authorities fed into the questionable narrative of western scientists and western media organizations on the origin and widespread transmission of the outbreak. Leading western journalists, like Laurie Garrett, who attributed the tide of infections and deaths in Sierra Leone to traditional burial practices, fail to explain how the government's national outbreak response, which

---

[159] Laurie Garrett, "Sierra Leone's Ebola Epidemic Is Spiraling Out of Control," *Foreign Policy Magazine*, December 10, 2014 (foreignpolicy.com/2014/12/10/sierra-leones-ebola-epidemic-is-spiraling-out-of-control).

criminalized diseases and African behavioral patterns, confounded the effectiveness of the health system and animated the agency of disease transmission. The case of Musu Massaquoi which was used by Garrett to justify the location of the outbreak's agency of transmission within the realms of African cultural behavior, for example, illustrates the epistemological insensitivity of western scientists and journalists to the victims of disaster, crisis, and disease in African society. Discussing the imprisonment of Musu Massaquoi by state authorities in Sierra Leone over the alleged violation of the national outbreak regulations, Garrett not only validated the criminalization of illness and proscription of victims (the real factors that actually animated the death and infection figures) but she also blamed the tragedy on the so-called backward behavioral patterns of the victims.

"Anyone who has lost a loved one can sympathize with Massaquoi's anguished misbehavior and pity her imprisonment. But epidemics call for drastic actions, and Massaquoi not only apparently violated safe burial procedures but, as a potential carrier of the virus herself, could have spread the disease to the people she attacked," Garrett stated, openly condemning the victim's act of protest and ultimately defending the obvious failure of the state's outbreak response strategy. What Garrett failed to highlight in the case of Musu Massaquoi, however, was how the state's ineffective outbreak response strategy created both the death of Musu Massaquoi's sister and the supposed resulting chain of transmission in the household; the government's ambulance team never showed up to transport Massaquoi's ailing sister after she was supposedly infected.

The essentiality of Musu Massaquoi's protest, an action criminalized both by the state's outbreak regulations and the epistemology of western reporters, was how the conflated disease response strategy of the Sierra Leone government – proscribing illness and criminalizing private medical care – animated the transmission agency of the outbreak and created the dual tragic circumstances of the Massaquoi family in Freetown. Western journalists, like Laurie Garrett, popularized the official narrative that widespread transmissions of the outbreak were due to community reluctance to give-up old cultural norms and behavioral patterns; families and victims were deliberately evading health care services and secretly burying their deceased relatives contrary to national laws and requirements of the outbreak. This narrative was not only a justification of the failed response strategy of national leaders, but it was a direct attack on African cultural behavioral patterns built out of a deliberate misconception and relegation of African culture and traditional norms and practices within the confines of savagery, barbarism, and primitivism.

On December 9, 2014, for example, the Council on Foreign Relations held a panel discussion on the Ebola crisis in Liberia and Sierra Leone moderated by *ABC's* health editor Richard Besser. It featured Nancy Aossey, president of the International Medical Corps, David Nabarro, the United Nations Special Envoy on Ebola, and Laurie Garrett, a senior fellow at the Council on Foreign Relations. During the conversation, Garrett was asked why Sierra Leone's outbreak was still out of control despite the robust measures adopted by national authorities. In response, Garrett blamed the explosion on "unsafe burials."

"The vast majority of burials are still unsafe," she said, adding that practices of preparing the dead for burial are rarely performed in funeral parlors or mortuaries but are executed by family members, who by doing so placed themselves at great risk for infection. Describing traditional funerals in Sierra Leone, Garrett claimed that they include cleansing the body inside and out, which according to her, also involves a process of "sitting the deceased in the home and people come and pay homage to the deceased, including hugging and kissing and talking to the deceased, and this can go on for a couple of days before the actual burial."[160]

This was not only a legitimation of official narratives on the transmission agency of the outbreak, but it is a classic example of the deliberate misrepresentation of African cultural behavior by western academics and journalists when discussing crisis, conflicts and disease in African society. Garrett's description is completely unreflective of the demographic and ethnographic arrangements of the country. Most of Sierra Leone's population of six million people is either Islamic or Christian in faith; over sixty percent are Muslims and more than twenty percent are Christian.[161] While claims of traditional religious beliefs reportedly exist in Sierra Leone, the statistics, regardless of exaggerations, do not exceed seven percent of the total population. Religious demographic behavioral trends in Sierra Leone are largely influenced by either Muslim religious culture or Christian religious beliefs and practices. Arabic and European religious beliefs and practices largely inform socio-cultural trends and behavior in Sierra Leone. Beliefs in life and death, burials, marriage, divorce, naming ceremonies, education, prayers, charity, sacrifice, dress codes, and social behavior in general all predominantly reflect either an Euro-American influence or an Arabian or Mediterranean influence. This is the direct impact and legacy of a dual cultural colonialism from Arabia and Europe. In Sierra Leone today, for instance, Imams and Clergies formalize most marriages regardless of whether they are conducted in Mosques or Churches or in family homes. Likewise, the majority of funeral services are also performed in Mosques or Churches and officiated by religious heads of these denominations.[162] In Muslim homes, the burials of corpses normally occur within the first

---

[160] Council on Foreign Relations Panel Discussion, "On-the-Ground Views of the Ebola Crisis in Liberia and Sierra Leone" held on December 9, 2014. See for additional information: www.cfr.org/diseases-infectious/--ground-views-ebola-crisis-liberia-sierra-leone/p35805.

[161] See Report of 2004 Housing and Population Census of Sierra Leone. For additional information also see, Population Division of the Department of Economic and Social Affairs of the United Nations Secretariat, World Population Prospects: The 2010 Revision. Additional information can also be found in the report, "Sierra Leone (02/08)". US Department of State. Retrieved July 15, 2015.

[162] 'Sierra Leone," *Worldmark Encyclopedia of Nations*, 2007, Encyclopedia.com, Web. 19 Sept. 2015 (www.

twenty-four hours of passing, which accordingly corresponds to the requirements of the Islamic faith that forbids keeping the remains of a dead family member. In cases where a deceased happen to be a Christian, corpses are either kept in mortuaries or funeral homes. This is also done to allow distant family members an opportunity to mobilize the required human and material resources to offer a plump funeral ceremony to the deceased. These services are usually performed in Churches and mostly common among members of the Creole community in Freetown. These events are devoid of any acts of "sitting the dead, or hugging, kissing and talking to the deceased," as described by Laurie Garrett.

Christianity and Islam still exercise a strong colonizing cultural influence in Sierra Leone (most public events in Sierra Leone, including government functions, start with Christian and Muslim prayers jointly recited by members from both religious denominations). Therefore, Garrett's claim that the lines "between ancient traditions that predate the arrival of Christianity and Islam, and local interpretations of the precepts of those established religions" are blurred does not reflect the prevailing ethnographical behavior of the country and, therefore, cannot be used as a premise to establish the transmission agency of the "2014 Ebola outbreak."

In actual reality, what cannot be distinguished in Sierra Leone, contrary to Garrett's claim, is the line between Christianity and Islam. The United States Department of State's 2013 International Religious Report, for instance, states that religion does not play a role in either ethnic or political identity in Sierra Leone. "Intermarriage among Christians and Muslims was common, and many families had both Christian and Muslim members living in the same household. Most citizens celebrate all religious holidays, regardless of sect or denomination, both at home and in houses of worship,"[163] the report noted. The same report, released a year before the outbreak in Sierra Leone, estimated the religious demography of the country to be around seventy-seven percent Muslim and twenty-one percent Christian. It is therefore questionable where and how Garrett observed the burial practices of "sitting the dead, or hugging, kissing and talking to the deceased" in a country largely influenced by foreign religious beliefs (Islam and Christianity) both of which reject such expressions towards the dead. In fact, the behavioral tendency of the urban majority of Sierra Leonean youth (including worldviews on music, dance, dress codes and lifestyles regardless of religious orientations) are largely driven by a colonizing Euro-American social culture which can also be largely attributed to modernizing advancements in technology, communication patterns, globalization, and media socialization. Therefore, the conclusion and reports of Garrett and other western journalists that traditional burial practices

---

encyclopedia.com/doc/1G2-2586700122.html).

[163] International Religious Freedom Report for 2013 of the United States Department of State, Bureau of Democracy, Human Rights and Labor. See: www.state.gov/documents/organization/222305.pdf.

in Sierra Leone served as an auxiliary to the transmission agency of the outbreak were predicated on a problematic sociological framework whose premise does not scientifically account for the widespread infections and deaths that occurred in Sierra Leone, especially between October and December 2014, a time when the militarized national response strategy of the government, backed and led mainly by army and police officers, had effectively proscribed private funerals and private medical care across the country.

Garrett's report is not only an example of the attack on African cultural behavior, but it is a complete misrepresentation of African behavioral patterns. Garrett, like the many western journalists who went to West Africa during the outbreak, appeared to have arrived with a predetermined reporting manual: a Eurocentric script which viewed African culture and social behavior – traditional communal ways of living and community relationship to the environment – as the central causative factors for understanding both the origin of the outbreak and its transmission agency. These are not only theoretically and scientifically misleading, but they present a seriously problematic challenge towards a real understanding of problematic global events and developments especially in so-called third world countries.

Like Robert Kaplan and Fabian Leendertz, Laurie Garrett's discourse on epidemiology in Africa, with specific reference to the 2014 outbreak in West Africa, reinforces Eurocentric views on the so-called role of "African cultural behavior and civilization" to the causes of disease, crisis and underdevelopment in Africa. In particular, Garrett's description of burial practices in Sierra Leone as a disease transmission agency is not only wrong, but it also depicts the centuries old image of Africa that western academics and journalists have constantly sold to their misinformed audiences in Europe and America. It is a narrow image that perpetually portrays Africa as a vast jungle of poverty, diseases, death, and corruption populated by starving children with swollen bellies; a place lacking hope and always requiring the goodwill of foreign philanthropies.

This approach towards Africa, a discourse conditioned by colonial constrictions, evokes what Samira Sawlani calls "philanthropic colonialism."[164] Writing on the online platform of *Media Diversified* in September 2013, Sawlani,[165] a scholar from the School of Oriental and African Studies in London, raised a fundamental issue: how the relationship between the new age of western charity, philanthropy

---

[164] Philanthropic colonialism is borrowed from an opinion article written by Peter Buffet in the *New York Times* of July 26, 2013 titled, "The Charitable-Industrial Complex," in which he expressed dissatisfaction with the new trend of philanthropic operations in Africa. For additional information see: www.nytimes.com/2013/07/27/opinion/the-charitable-industrial-complex.html, Web. 5 September 2015.

[165] Samira Sawlani is a UK based writer specializing in politics, economics, and development of East and Horn of Africa, in particular Kenya, Uganda, and Somalia. She served as an International Election Observer for the Kenyan elections in 2013.

and the western media's stereotypical portrayal of Africa represents the new brand of colonialism in Africa.

"Voodoo, scammers, corrupt leaders, slums, poverty, hungry people, drums, polygamy, lawlessness, child soldiers; the list of how Africa is depicted in popular culture and the media goes on,"[166] Sawlani wrote. She adds that, "Africa seems to hold a certain image, almost as if it has been assigned a particular role, which it has to fill in every sphere be it in academia, media, international relations, politics and business."

Sawlani noted that the stereotypical images, which western journalists associate with Africa, could mostly not be identified with any one particular country. "Africa has become the umbrella term, a continent which through sweeping generalizations becomes the bearer of every type of misery, ailment and joy which any one of the countries within it experiences," she stated. But Sawlani, however, is not alone in the growing frustrations against the western media's coverage of Africa that often portrays the continent as "one huge warzone of barren earth, potholed roads and a people with their hands held out asking for money." In February 2012, for instance, Kathryn Mathers of Duke University wrote an amazing critique of the award-wining *New York Times* columnist and blogger, Nicholas Kristof's reporting on Africa. In an article titled, "Mr. Kristof, I Presume?"[167] Mathers examined how Kristof's columns in the *New York Times* are filled with poorly researched material and blatant generalizations that represents Africa with sheer banality.

Mathers said Kristof's writings helps to repeat "troubling and problematic tropes about Africa" and makes him "part of the astonishingly wide range of people participating in cementing a peculiarly colonial set of images and ideas about Africa." According to Mathers, the contemporary images of Africa and engagement with Africans put out by western journalists and reporters are reminiscent of the ways the continent was imagined and fashioned in imperial and colonial times in Europe and America. Indeed, these contemporary images of Africa flow down from the travel diaries of early fourteenth century European navigators like Mungo Park and Christopher Columbus to personal accounts of colonialist conquerors like Henry Stanley, Lotta von Trotta and Cecil Rhodes.

These invented images of Africa are still reinforced in the writings of the many western reporters, including Robert Kaplan, Nicholas Kristof, and Laurie Garrett, who today occupy authoritative positions among western academia regardless of the sweeping generalizations evident in their travel writings on Africa. Their style of reportage not only continues to portray Africa as an untamed wilderness

---

[166] Samira Sawlani, "Charity, Philanthropy and Media Stereotypes: Africa's new colonialists?" *Media Diversified*, September 20, 2013 (mediadiversified.org/2013/09/20/charity-philanthropy-media-stereotypes-africas-new-colonialists).

[167] See: Kathryn Mathers, "Mr. Kristof I Presume" (www.academia.edu/2090911/Mr_Kristof_I_Presume).

devoid of markers of modernity and global connections, but, as Mathers puts it, they present African people "either as backdrops to the Westerners adventures and discovery, or as embodiments of primevalness; helpless characters in travelers stories about self-discovery and responsibility." And the 2014 outbreak in West Africa provided a great opportunity to western journalists and scientists, like Fabian Leendertz and Laurie Garrett, to implement their atrocious reporting and portrayal of "Africa's backwardness" and African people's cultural existence as antagonistic factors to health, environmental protection and economic development. Western epistemologies that locate disease, poverty and crisis in Africa on African cultural factors and behavioral patterns do not only offer a bias and misleading analysis and understanding of African society, but they simultaneously stigmatize the image of Africa and the true identity of African people.

In the case of the West African Ebola outbreak, such epistemological approaches not only blamed the causes of the outbreak on its African victims, but they also significantly altered, stigmatized, and helped to proscribe the image and identity of the victims of the epidemic. Both the western scientific narrative on the origin of the outbreak and the western media coverage of its so-called agency of transmission, including its accompanying atrocities, were based on the criminalization of African cultural behavior and the stigmatization of African identity (the dual act of blaming and proscribing a victim for circumstances beyond his/her control and comprehension). Therefore, as Mathers puts it, Africa is now a place where western academics and journalists go to learn and report about the limits of modernity. And West Africa, which Kaplan regarded in 1994 as an epitome of what the political character of the world would become in the twenty-first century,[168] now remains perpetually trapped between these violent theoretical and physical contradictions produced by the predatory Euro-American economic forces and their permanent allies of intentionally-bias epistemologists.

---

[168] See Robert D. Kaplan's 1994 article, "The Coming Anarchy" published by *The Atlantic Monthly*.

CONCLUSION

POST-EBOLA RECOVERY: ISSUES OF HUMAN RIGHTS, JUSTICE, AND REPARATIONS

Genocide means any of the following acts committed with intent to destroy, in whole or in part, a national, ethnical, racial or religious group, such as killing members of the group; causing serious bodily or mental harm to members of the group; deliberately inflicting on the group conditions of life calculated to bring about its physical destruction in whole or in part...

– Convention on the Prevention and Punishment of the Crime of Genocide[169]

The Kailahun Ebola Test Controversy

On April 4, 2015, a serious controversy erupted in Kailahun district in the eastern region of Sierra Leone. It involved a dispute between opposition politician Alex Bonapha and district health officials in Kailahun, regarding the test result of a deceased child.[170]

The child, a nine-month-old baby, died at the Nixon Memorial Hospital in Segbwema on April 3, 2015. A few days before the tragic incident, doctors at the hospital had recommended a blood transfusion for the child. An uncle is said to have donated the blood given to the child. The baby passed away just hours after the blood was transfused. Health officials, who conducted a swab test at the Ebola Management Center in Kailahun, later claimed that the child died a victim

---

[169] Excerpted from Article 2 of the *Convention on the Prevention and Punishment of the Crime of Genocide*. The United Nations General Assembly Resolution 260 passed on December 9, 1948. They adopted the measure, and it entered into active force on January 12, 1951.

[170] "Ebola: The More We Learn, the More We Realize How Much We Don't Know," *Sewa News*, April 4, 2015 (sewanews.blogspot.com/2015/04/ebola-more-we-learn-more-we-realize-how.html).

of the Ebla virus. Officials from the National Ebola Response Center (NERC) in Freetown recommended that Kailahun district be closed down and the family of the deceased child be quarantined. Kailahun was the initial site of the outbreak a year before and had gone almost two months without a single reported infection at the time of the child's death.

Alex Bonapha, the district council chairman in the area, instantly challenged the validity of the child's Ebola test result and protested against the NERC's decision to re-quarantine the district. Bonapha asserted that the child's test result shed doubt on the whole Ebola management system.

"We are strongly contesting the validity of the one case today in Kailahun," Bonapha said in a statement issued in response to the child's test result. "For a person to be infected, he or she has to come in contact with an already infected person or must have touched the vomits, urine, saliva, excreta or the sweat of an infected person," he also stated, arguing that the deceased child was not exposed to any of these required risks of infection.

According to Bonapha, all members of the child's family, including the mother who was breastfeeding the child and the uncle who reportedly donated the blood that was given to the child, were Ebola negative and never infected before the child's death.

"All the family members of the late child including the mother are very healthy and alive. If the child got (Ebola) from the mother, the mother would first have manifested symptoms before transmission, but this was not the case. The child could not have got the virus through breastfeeding because the mother is neither an Ebola survivor, nor has she up to now manifested any signs or symptoms. The uncle of the child who donated his blood has stayed in Segbwema for over nine weeks without leaving the town and he is also not a survivor," he argued in his widely circulated protest statement.

Bonapha then demanded that frontline responders to the outbreak in Sierra Leone (the National Ebola Response Center (NERC), the World Health Organization (WHO), and UNICEF) explain how the test result of the child turned out to be Ebola positive when the child was not exposed to any of the conditions that cause the infection.

"My suspicion is that either the swab result was interchanged, or the blood that was donated for the child was reserved in the blood bank (while) another from the same blood group, as the one donated by the uncle, was used on the child," he stated.

Bonapha's protest was more than a political action from an opposition council chairman fighting to protect his constituents from the harsh disease quarantine measures enforced by troops of central government officials in Freetown. His protest raised a fundamental question about the outbreak: what was the actual transmission mode of the virus?

A fierce debate erupted between Alex Bonapha and the district health officials. The health officials received support from ruling party propagandists.[171]

Government propagandists tried to dismiss Bonapha's statement and position on the matter, calling it inflammatory and inciting. As council chairman, Alex Bonapha had been at the center of controversy with officials of the Koroma administration and he remained one of the strongest opposition critics of the central government's response to the outbreak. Responding to Bonapha, Sylvia Olayinka Blyden, a former presidential assistant and owner of the pro-Koroma *Awareness Times* newspaper, stated that the child's test result could either be the result of the mother or the uncle being asymptomatic carriers of the Ebola virus.

"The child's swab test should be re-run or if the corpse is already buried, for the body to be exhumed and another swab test be collected and re-run," Blyden suggested, but stated that the child's "mother and entire family must in the interim be subjected to twenty-one days quarantine."

The controversy over the child's death now threatened the credibility of the entire Ebola response effort. Kailahun district itself had gone from being a leading Ebola hotspot, with nearly eighty infections per week in June 2014, to exhibiting zero cases for a consecutive period of over one hundred days before the controversial diagnoses of the deceased child. But despite the sanguinary response of government propagandists, Alex Bonapha still insisted that the result did not reflect the deceased child's Ebola status. The arguments eventually forced the United Nations agencies involved in the Ebola response efforts and the country's National Ebola Response Center (NERC) to conduct an investigation into the circumstances of the child's death and the test result.

An investigation team, made up of representatives from the Sierra Leone health ministry, WHO, and the United States Center for Disease Control (CDC), was then constituted in Freetown and dispatched to Kailahun to undertake the investigation. The investigation team later discovered that there was strong basis for Alex Bonapha's protest: they found no evidence that there was an ongoing Ebola transmission in Kailahun and that the child in question was not an Ebola case.

"The sample in question is not from the child,"[172] the team tacitly stated in its report.

NERC officials in Freetown later called the controversy surrounding the child "a mere mistake," which they blamed on a lower ranking Ebola health worker. Alex Bonapha, the council chairman who raised the sensitive question, appeared

---

[171] Kemoh Cham, "Sierra Leone Rules Baby's Ebola Test a Mistake," *Africa Reviews*, April 8, 2015 (www.africareview.com/News/Sierra-Leone-rules-a-babys-Ebola-test-a-mistake/-/979180/2679398/-/view/printVersion/-/1f756r/-/index.html).

[172] "Kailahun Baby Was Not Ebola Positive – Says NERC's Paolo Conteh," *Sierra Leone Telegraph*, April 7, 2015 (www.thesierraleonetelegraph.com/?p=9086).

to have scored a significant political victory against his opponents.

"We want NERC to offer a public apology as a way of restoring confidence with the people of the district. Many people are now afraid to go to the hospital," Bonapha told the *Politico* newspaper in Freetown.

The government propagandists, who called Bonapha's protest "immature and inflammatory," immediately changed the focus of the discussion. They quickly subsumed Bonapha's protest and replaced the matter with praises for the joint investigators.

The *Sierra Leone Telegraph* praised what it called, "The encouragingly unprecedented speed with which the ministry of health, NERC and the international health agencies in the country responded to the community's call for answers."

The controversial matter regarding the child's test result was closed. But underneath the torrent of accusations and counter-accusations between the politicians and health officials there still remains a fundamental question: was the child's test result a real mistake? Many people wondered how many of such "mistakes" may have occurred during the outbreak. The question as to how the said "mistake" actually happened was never exhausted. Alex Bonapha and the child's family members never pursued the matter any further.

The Myth of Mammie Lebbie's Survival Story

The Kailahun incident of April 2015 was neither a coincidental case nor a unique occurrence. It is one example in the thousands of cases that the troops of western journalists and many in the African media, stamped below the surface in their inundated media coverage of the outbreak and its casualties. In the very same district of Kailahun, there also exists the story of Mammie Lebbie, a 39-year old peasant woman in a village called Sokoma near the southeastern border with Guinea. Mammie Lebbie is a daughter-in-law to Mendinor, the traditional healer whom officials initially considered the index case in Sierra Leone. Mammie was supposedly diagnosed with Ebola at the Koindu Community Health Center on May 24, 2014, after she and other women are said to have participated in the funeral rites of Mendinor. When Mrs. Lebbie became ill, an Ebola swab collector and contact tracer named Mohamed Lamin (who was stationed at the Koindu Community Health Center) reportedly collected her urine and stool specimen, which were taken to the Kenema Government Hospital's Lassa Fever Ward. On that day, a medical doctor named Kanneh reportedly administered ten intravenous fluids to Mrs. Lebbie. Mrs. Lebbie arrived at the Koindu health center in a weak and dehydrated condition after walking a distance of two miles from her village. Meanwhile, laboratory workers at the Kenema Government Hospital's Lassa Fever Ward confirmed the following day that Mammie Lebbie's urine samples tested positive for the Ebola virus. They requested that she and all the other patients (a total of ten) at the Koindu Health Center should be relocated to the

Kenema Government Hospital's Lassa Fever Ward, which had been transformed into the new Ebola Holding Center. This was on May 25, 2014, the very day the government of Sierra Leone officially announced the presence of the Ebola virus in the country. The test result of Mrs. Lebbie then became the first supposed laboratory confirmed infection of the outbreak in Sierra Leone.

But when report of the test result was conveyed to Mammie Lebbie and she was told of plans to relocate her to the isolation ward in Kenema, she and other patients reportedly fled from the clinic. They fled the night before an ambulance team from Kenema arrived in Koindu to transfer them. On May 26, 2014, health officials and local authorities in the area declared Mammie Lebbie a "wanted Ebola patient" and a search for her arrest was launched in Kailahun. She eventually fled to Guinea and was arrested by health officials at a local clinic in the Gueckedou area where she attempted to seek medical care. Health officials were making arrangements to repatriate her to Kenema when she re-escaped and then fled back to Sierra Leone. When she arrived at her village, her husband, a 49-year old man named Tamba Lebbie, immediately took her to an abandoned farmhouse in the bush where she remained in hiding for more than a month. She resurfaced towards the end of June 2014. By this time, Mammie Lebbie had fully recovered from her ailment without any treatment.

Mammie Lebbie returned to Sokoma with both her husband and six children. In January 2015, a group of journalists who heard about her story met with Lebbie to interview her and also arranged for another Ebola test to be conducted. The test result came back negative. Lebbie was then issued a survivor's certificate and identified as the first Ebola survivor in Sierra Leone. But the journalists and the health officials ignored the fact that Mammie Lebbie was never treated for Ebola after she reportedly tested positive for the virus. She had been on the run since the initial diagnosis. None of her family members, including her husband who was in direct contact with her during her days in hiding, were infected or fell ill. She had recovered from the virus with no professional treatment, and the family members who cared for her had avoided infection despite taking no containment measures.

Health officials ignored the most significant aspects that characterized Mrs. Lebbie's status as a so-called Ebola survivor. In fact, a few weeks after she was officially identified as Sierra Leone's first survivor, her story was re-invented: she became a poster for the possibility of survival from Ebola when one seeks medical care immediately after infection. Sadly, the journalists who assisted in the identification of Mrs. Lebbie as Sierra Leone's first Ebola survivor never questioned the circumstances of her survival. The journalists also failed to question whether her supposed test result, which was used by national officials to announce the presence of the virus in Sierra Leone, was actually clinically accurate.

Mammie Lebbie remains an unresolved puzzle: the absence of an independent clinical verification of her test results, the absence of a medical or scientific justification of the circumstances of her survival, and the fact that her unprotected husband and six children were not infected remains a critical component of the evidence against both the origin and transmission narratives of the outbreak.

Patient Zero's Unresolved Questions

Mrs. Lebbie's puzzling story equally mirrors the controversial circumstances surrounding the identification of Emile Ouamouno of Miliandou as the index case of the outbreak in West Africa.[173]

The report of German scientists, led by Fabian Leendertz, which supposedly identified the cause of the outbreak and its primary infection, omitted significant aspects of the child who they called "patient zero" of the outbreak. The evidence which identified Emile Ouamouno as the first Ebola victim in West Africa was not based on clinical tests: no laboratory examination was carried out on the child's remains or any of his specimen to determine his actual cause of death. Available medical records of the child at the community health clinic in Miliandou only state that the child was diagnosed with acute malaria in December 2013. Local health workers still think malaria may have been the actual cause of his death. Malaria is indeed an endemic disease in southern Guinea and is the leading cause of infant deaths in the region.[174] Other vital records available on Emile Ouamouno at the Miliandou health clinic also confirmed that the child was eighteen months old at the time of his death. This contradicts information provided by German scientists who identified Emile as two-years-old. The age discrepancy also challenges the logic of the child's supposed ability to participate in the activities of hunting and grilling of the "insectivorous bats" circumstantially identified by Leendertz and team as the infection source of the virus. Additionally, if Leendertz's circumstantial scenario were accurate, wouldn't it be natural to consider that the child might have participated in the bat-hunting activity with other older children? Unfortunately, the Robert Koch Institute's report provided no information of other children who may have been playmates to eighteen-month-old Emile and who likely would have also participated in the activity of "child bat hunting" that killed Emile and eventually sparked the deadly disaster in the region.

Also ignored by scientists and journalists are the circumstances that surrounded the death of Emile's mother and the survival of his father. Emile's immediate senior sister died around the same time as him. Emile's mother was eight months pregnant at the time of her children's death. The mother reportedly fell ill a few days after the funeral of the two children. A doctor at the community health clinic in the village who treated Emile also diagnosed the mother with

---

[173] See the RKI report of Fabian Leendertz and colleagues cited extensively in Chapter 1: "Investigating the Zoonotic Origin of West Africa's Ebola Epidemic."

[174] See statistical data in Chapter 7 and the WHO report on global deaths resulting from malaria also cited in Chapter 7.

malaria. The doctor prescribed ten injections. She complained of severe hip pains the very night she commenced the treatment prescribed by the doctor. The hip pains later developed into severe bleeding, and in the middle of the night the woman eventually miscarried and died in a pool of blood. The circumstances of the woman's death, an eight month old pregnant woman receiving anti-malarial injections, suffering severe hip pains followed by profuse bleeding, then having a miscarriage and eventually dying, makes her a potential statistic of the high incidences of maternal deaths prevalent in the region.

Significantly, the German scientists who identified Emile Ouamouno as the outbreak's primary victim buried a critical aspect of their findings: they provided no explanation on the local doctor who treated both Emile Ouamouno and his mother and how he was able to escape infection. They also deliberately failed to explain why Etienne Ouamouno, the child's father who took care of all the so-called index cases of the outbreak (the child and his sister and mother), was not infected and did not report a fever or suffer any illness throughout the outbreak. They also failed to explain how the child's other siblings (Victorienne 8 years old, Sergio 7 years old, Marie 6 years old, and Kanih 18 months old) were also never infected, despite the fact that the outbreak, which spread across international borders and killed thousands, allegedly erupted in their household.

An examination of these contentious episodes – from the death of Emile Ouamouno in Miliandou to Mammie Lebbie's survival story in Koindu – unravels a trail of undocumented testimonies of clinical wrongdoings, questionable scientific claims, and misleading media reports on the outbreak's origin and modes of transmission. Underneath these questionable stories lie the un-discussed predicaments of the outbreak's many victims. All across the Mano River countries in West Africa today, communities harbor telling stories that are much more contentious and frightening. In their totality, these stories not only cast severe doubts over the origin of the outbreak and its modes of transmission, but like the so-called mistaken test result of the Kailahun child of April 2015, they tell real-time stories of suspicious deaths, of hundreds of doubtful infections, of strange and unknown disease treatment methods, and of many other ethical issues involving medical experts practicing beyond the parameters of informed consent. These chilling accounts of the victims, of the families of the deceased, of the survivors – real firsthand accounts from true eye-witnesses – have been largely dismissed by scientists and political leaders, oftentimes regarded as "conspiracy theory" in the western and African medias. But these subsumed and suppressed firsthand accounts contain cold and sad recollections of events that are too frightening, too rampant, and too commonplace to be ignored. They cannot be swept under the rug. As incredible as they sound, as unbelievable as scientists and journalists want them to appear, they form an important part of evidence in any genuine effort geared towards a real understanding of the motives and outcomes of the 2014

West African tragedy.

The Unrecognizable Complications of Recovery

On October 14, 2015, British doctors issued a shocking announcement: they reported that a British nurse named Pauline Cafferkey, who suffered complications from an Ebola infection she supposedly contracted while working as a volunteer in Sierra Leone nearly a year earlier, had been re-hospitalized at the Royal Free Hospital in London.

Cafferkey had been cured of the virus back in January 2015, after spending a month in hospital. British newspapers reported that the news of Cafferkey's worsening condition was shocking to medical experts in Britain.

"While it is recognized that the virus can linger in parts of the body after a patient has recovered, it has never before been known to trigger potentially lethal disease months after the initial illness," *The Guardian* newspaper stated in a news article announcing the event.[175]

A professor of molecular virology at the University of Nottingham, Jonathan Ball, described the news as "staggering."

"I am not aware from the scientific literature of a case where Ebola has been associated with what we can only assume as life-threatening complications after someone has initially recovered, and certainly not so many months after," Prof. Ball told *The Guardian* newspaper in London.

Cafferkey's story is an example of the complicated fate of the thousands of people in Sierra Leone, Liberia, and Guinea now considered "Ebola survivors." Many of them have developed unrecognized complications like blindness and deafness, and some have even died of other unknown adverse side-effects months after their so-called recovery.

Apart from these complicated health conditions, West Africa's "Ebola survivors" are also exposed to conditions of exploitation and stigma.

On October 4, 2015, in Sierra Leone, for example, the *Politico* newspaper reported a heart-rending story relating to a group of "Ebola survivors."[176] The newspaper reported that some survivors in the Waterloo-Lumpa community in the rural districts of Freetown had refused to attend an Ebola education campaign because the organizers of the event, a children's organization named Kids Advocacy Network, had not paid them for their participation. The survivors also alleged that the organization wanted to use them as fundraising bait. The organizers denied the allegations and said the event was part of a campaign against

---

[175] Sarah Boseley, "Ebola nurse Pauline Cafferkey Critically Ill in Deterioration that Shocks Sxperts," *The Guardian*, October 14, 2015 (www.theguardian.com/world/2015/oct/14/ebola-nurse-pauline-cafferkey-critically-ill).

[176] Mustapha Sesay, "Sierra Leone Ebola Survivors Demand Money," *Politico*, October 5, 2015 (politicosl.com/2015/05/sierra-leone-ebola-survivors-demand-money).

stigmatization of "Ebola survivors and orphans."

The Waterloo-Lumpa incident, reported by *Politico*, clearly illustrates what is now called the "post-Ebola" challenges confronting local politicians and community leaders in the Mano River countries of West Africa. An environment of deep-seated mistrust, the fear and suspicion that now characterize relations between community leaders and national politicians are directly related to the questionable events surrounding the outbreak and its management. Communal eyebrows have remained raised over the massive theft of the outbreak's emergency funds and the way rogue politicians utilized the catastrophe to accumulate stolen wealth. These are just part of the many ugly developments that continually cast doubts on nearly every program, regardless of real intensions, aimed at victims and survivors in the region.

These contradictions, the lack of faith in community leaders, the pervasive deep-seated mistrust for national politicians, and the general suspicion now prevailing across affected communities in the region, are the direct results of a number of unexplained events during the outbreak. The developments, which have heightened community distrust and suspicion towards all local, national, and international interventions in West Africa, need to be investigated and cleared. The story of the 2014 outbreak, its questionable origin and modes of transmission, and how certain individuals and organizations profited from the disaster and deaths that occurred in West Africa, must be looked into in the interest of justice, peace, and human dignity. A clear path towards recovery must begin with uncovering the truth: an independent investigation that employs the services of forensics and victim testimonies has to be considered as part of a genuine healing process and as a bulwark for preventing the recurrence of crimes against humanity and genocide.

Reconciling the Past with the Present

On July 11, 2005, in a message marking the tenth anniversary of the Srebrenica genocide, Kofi Annan, then secretary general of the United Nations, attempted to address a crucial aspect in international justice: the extent to which international powers can be morally and physically held responsible for either directly or indirectly fomenting, condoning, or failing to prevent the escalation of events with a potential to destroy humanity and global peace.

"It is undeniable that blame lies, first and foremost, with those who planned and carried out the massacre, or who assisted them, or who harbored and are harboring them still. But we cannot evade our own share of responsibility," Kofi Annan stated. He noted that the human catastrophe in Srebrenica would have been avoided had the United Nations acted swiftly to prevent the events that developed into the massacre. "We can say, and it is true, that great nations failed to respond adequately," Annan admitted, acknowledging that, "the tragedy of

Srebrenica will haunt our history forever."

Kofi Annan suggested that to address crimes of the past, the world should ensure that systematic slaughter does not reoccur anywhere in the present or future. This entails that the actors can be guilty not just for committing genocide, but also for allowing it to happen.

"The world must equip itself to act collectively against genocide, ethnic cleansing and crimes against humanity," Annan emphasized.

It is obvious that efforts to draw up historical comparisons between the Srebrenica massacre and the human catastrophe of the Mano River countries in 2014 might raise arguments about the similarity of the events with regards to their unique geographic and socio-political contexts. Nevertheless, there exists within the parameters of the historical cases of genocide and the spirit of international criminal justice a common applicable procedure and trajectory for determining crimes against humanity and genocide. In the case of the 2014 West African outbreak, such a determination can start with an investigation (within the realms of the applicability of the *Nuremberg Code*[177] and its possible violation) into the historical events that created both the conditions for the outbreak and its agency of transmission. This could be a first step to uncover and confront what Kofi Annan calls, "the full truth about what happened" in the West African countries of Sierra Leone, Liberia, and Guinea. A process of reconciling the past with the present in the interest of a peaceful future must start with a genuine process of justice. Without justice, there will be no peace for the families of the victims. Without trust, the requisites for national economic development and collective social progress can never be attained.

---

[177] The Nuremberg Code is a set of research ethics and principles for human experimentation set as a result of the Subsequent Nuremberg Trials at the end of the Second World War. The trails looked at the crimes committed by German doctors who carried out the genocidal medical experiments against Jews and other populations during the Second World War.

ACKNOWLEDGEMENTS

On March 29, 2015, I arrived at JFK International Airport in New York on board an *Iberian Airline* flight from Dakar, Senegal. It was my first journey to America since the outbreak began in West Africa. I started my trip in Conakry two days earlier. At the airport in Conakry I filled-out a questionnaire with a number of questions and my temperature was taken multiple times; I showed no signs of a fever or any of the symptoms consistent with the Ebola virus. Every time I received a temperature check in West Africa I was frightened. I had been traveling extensively across communities affected by the outbreak whilst doing my research, and I was very tired and exhausted. I feared the unreliability of the temperature checks at most locations. At the airport, though, I was issued a clearance to board the regional flight from Conakry to Dakar. I went through the same procedures at the airport in Senegal before I boarded the flight to Madrid. I was suspiciously eyed each time I showed my passport to Spanish immigration police at the airport. I spent five hours in transit before leaving for New York. I had asked a friend from Sierra Leone to pick me up at JFK. On arrival, US customs and border inspection officials took me to a room where my temperature was checked again and a marathon of questions was asked. All questions related to whether I had been close to an Ebola patient or a deceased person. I was then presented with a telephone and a thermometer to check and report my temperature each morning to the Center for Disease Control (CDC) and sent on my way.

I came out of the terminal and my friend who had agreed to pick me up was nowhere to be found. I made countless phone calls to other friends, and with each phone call came a repeated assurance that someone would come and get me. I waited for more than three hours and no one came. It appeared all those I called were scared of the virus due to the stigma resulting from hysterical western media coverage of the outbreak and the incidental cases that appeared in the United States. I spent the night at a hotel near the airport through the intervention of another comrade who lived in a different city. For the next twenty-one days the CDC kept track of me, calling me to check my daily temperature until they were satisfied that I was not a potential Ebola patient.

The publication of this book has, therefore, not been easy. It has been made possible through the active support and encouragement received from many individuals whose contributions, comments, and suggestions were extremely useful.

I hereby express profound appreciation to my friend and senior brother, Kalilu Ibrahim Totangi for his continued support and suggestions throughout the process of writing this book. I also thank the following people for the diverse support and assistance: Sulaiman Barrie, Edmond Abu, Prince Ahmed Abe Osagie, Edward Sundima Tiffa, all in Freetown; Alhaji C. Bah in Makeni; Binta Jalloh from Kabala; freelance journalist Baboucarr Ceesay in the Gambia, Helena Kamara in Miami; Hon. Mohamed Kakay and Nicole Harris in Philadelphia; Mark Klus of the Free Library of Philadelphia, Dr. Sayida Self of the Bronx Community College in New York, Prof. Nwenna Kai of Lincoln University, Dr. Lansana Kormoh in London; Mariama Yanka Timbo in Canada; Brother Omowale Rupert Charles of the Pan-Afrikan Society Community Forum in London; Comrade Natalio Sowande Wheatley of the British Virgin Islands; Comrade Omavi Bailey in Arizona; Ahmed Bah and Ibrahim Bah in New York.

I am extremely grateful for the continued support of Brother Cheikh Amma Diop in Maryland. During the Ebola outbreak, Brother Diop organized the *Rice for Sierra Leone Campaign*, an online fundraising initiative that successfully mobilized financial resources to purchase food for orphans and other victims in Sierra Leone during the many lockdowns and quarantines. I also wish to acknowledge the support I continue to receive from my brother and friend, Mohamed L. Bah, the president of the Fullah Progressive Union (FPU) in Maryland and executive director of Patriotic Care Sierra Leone. I also extend my appreciation to my good friends, Mona R. Washington in New Jersey, Liliana Sifuentes in Las Cruces, and Eileen deLespinase in Las Vegas.

During the research for this book, I benefitted immensely from discussions with Sierra Leonean freelance journalist Jaime Yayah Barrie, and from the often reliable advice and encouragement of veteran journalist, Pios Foray, proprietor of the *Democrat* newspaper – whose work and commitment to the cause of freedom and justice are always a source of inspiration and reference.

However, this work has been made possible only to a larger extent due to the exemplary role and support of my dear friends and comrades: Jessica Collen McDermott and Joshua Lew McDermott. Both individuals have supported this project from its conception unto its final completion, serving both as editors, readers, and research companions throughout the process. My family equally remains grateful to the immense support we continue to receive from Jessica and Joshua. During the months of April and May 2015, Joshua and Jessica helped organized a comprehensive speaking tour for me in New Mexico and Idaho. I benefited immensely from the many discussions with students and faculty in Las

Cruces, New Mexico and Moscow, Idaho. I hereby extend my thanks to the students and faculty at New Mexico State University in Las Cruces and the University of Idaho in Moscow who provided platforms for initial discussions on some of the issues addressed in this book.

In this regard, I also express great thanks and appreciation to the work of the African Socialist Movement (ASM) International Support Committee, and all our friends and allies across the world.

I also want to thank the tireless support of Comrade Matthew Willis in California for his unconditional contribution to my many initiatives and projects.

I wish to state that the credit for all the work that I do today belongs to my mother, Madam Lirwan Bah, whose influence continue to shape my thinking and understanding of humanity. I conclude by thanking my entire family for their continued support and understanding: My dear Isatu Bah, Allieu M. Bah, my sisters – Mariama and Lamarana – Alhaji S. Bah, Mohamed S. Jalloh, Abubakarr Bah, Alhassan and Alusine Jalloh; and the entire family. The list is too long to be mentioned.

My final word of appreciation goes to Dr. Lansana Gberie who offered the foreword to this book.

Freetown
October 15, 2015.

BIBLIOGRAPHY

Aigner, Dietrich (1985). *Hitler's Ultimate Aims – A Programme of World Dominion?*. In Koch, H.W. Aspects of the Third Reich. London: MacMillan.

Bah, Chernoh Alpha M. (2014). *Neocolonialism in West Africa: A Collection of Essays & Articles.* iUniverse: Bloomington.

Baranowski, Shelley (2011). *Nazi Empire: German Colonialism and Imperialism from Bismarck to Hitler.* Cambridge University Press.

Barnes, David S. (1995) *The Making of a Social Disease: Tuberculosis in Nineteenth-Century France.* University of California Press.

Barnes, David S. (2006) *The Great Stink of Paris and the Nineteenth-Century Struggle Against Filth and Germs.* The Johns Hopkins University Press; Oxford University Press.

Bauer, Yehuda (2000). *Rethinking the Holocaust.* Yale University Press.

Bausch, DG; Sesay, SS; Oshin, B (2004). *On The Front Lines of Lassa Fever. Emerging Infectious Diseases* 10 (10): 1889–1890.

Berewa, Solomon E. (2011) *A New Perspective On Governance, Leadership, Conflict And Nation Building In Sierra Leone.* London: Author House UK.

Black, Edwin (2004). *War Against the Weak: Eugenics and America's Campaign to Create a Master Race.* Thunder's Mouth Press.

Blaut, James Morris (1992). *Fourteen Ninety-Two: The Debate on Colonialism, Eurocentrism and History.* Trenton, NJ: Africa World Press.

Blaut, James Morris (1993). *The Colonizer's Model of the World: Geographical Diffusionism and Eurocentric History.* New York: Guilford Press.

Blautt, James Morris (2000). *Eight Eurocentric Historians.* New York: Guilford Press.

Carlyle, Thomas (1849). *Occasional Discourse on the Negro Question.* Fraser's Magazine for Town and Country, Vol. XL.

Cartwright, Samuel (1851). *Report on the Diseases and Peculiarities of the Negro Race.* DeBow's Review XI.

Chandler, Alice (1998). *Carlyle and the Medievalism of the North. In: Medievalism in the Modern World. Essays in Honour of Leslie J. Workman. Ed. Richard Utz and Tom*

Shippey. Turnhout: Brepols.

Clayton, David and Michael Hills (1993). *Statistical Models in Epidemiology.* Oxford University Press.

Darwin, Charles (1859). *On the Origin of Species by Means of Natural Selection, or the Preservation of Favoured Races in the Struggle for Life* (1st ed.). London: John Murray.

Darwin, Charles (1868). *The Variation of Animals and Plants under Domestication.* London: John Murray.

Darwin, Charles (1871). *The Descent of Man, and Selection in Relation to Sex* (1st ed.). London: John Murray.

Darwin, Charles; Wallace, Alfred Russel (1858). *On the Tendency of Species to form Varieties; and on the Perpetuation of Varieties and Species by Natural Means of Selection.* Journal of the Proceedings of the Linnean Society of London. Zoology 33 (9).

Donaldson, R. I. (2009). *The Lassa Ward: One Man's Fight Against One of the World's Deadliest Diseases.* New York, NY: St. Martin's Press.

Downing, David (2005). *The Nazi Death Camps.* World Almanac Library of the Holocaust.

Evans, Richard J. (2003). *The Coming of the Third Reich.* New York: Penguin Group.

Evans, Richard J. (2005). *The Third Reich in Power.* New York: Penguin Group.

Evans, Richard J. (2008). *The Third Reich At War.* New York: Penguin Group.

Fischer, E. and H.F.K. Günther. (1927) *Deutsche Köpfe nordischer Rasse: 50 Abbildungen mit Geleitwarten.* Munich: J.F. Lehmann.

Fischer, Eugen (1899) *Beiträge zur Kenntniss der Nasenhöhle und des Thränennasenganges der Amphisbaeniden.* Archiv für Mikroskopische Anatomie.

Fischer, Eugen (1901) *Zur Kenntniss der Fontanella metopica und ihrer Bildungen.* Zeitschrift für Morphologie und Anthropologie.

Fischer, Eugen (1913) *Die Rehobother Bastards und das Bastardierungsproblem beim Menschen: anthropologische und ethnographiesche Studien am Rehobother Bastardvolk in Deutsch-Südwest-Afrika, ausgeführt mit Unterstützung der Kgl.* preuss, Akademie der Wissenschaften.

Frame JD, Baldwin JM, Gocke DJ, Troup JM (1970). *Lassa Fever, A New Virus Disease of Man from West Africa.* I. Clinical Description and Pathological Findings. Am. J. Tropical Medical Hygiene. 19 (4): 670–6.

Frank Robert Chalk, Kurt Jonassohn (1990) *The History and Sociology of Genocide: Analyses and Case Studies.* Montreal Institute for Genocide Studies. Yale University Press.

Friedlander, Henry (1997). *The origins of Nazi genocide: From Euthanasia to the Final Solution.* University of North Carolina Press.

Garrett, Laurie (1995). *The Coming Plague: Newly Emerging Diseases in a World Out of Balance.* Penguin.

Garrett, Laurie (2001). *Betrayal of Trust: The Collapse of Global Public Health.* Hyperion.

Garrett, Laurie (2011). *I Heard the Sirens Scream: How Americans Responded to the 9/11 and Anthrax Attacks.* Amazon.com Kindle e-book.

Gould, S. J. (1978). *Morton's Ranking of Races by Cranial Capacity.* Science 200 (May 5).

Harrold, Charles Frederick (1934). *Carlyle and German Thought: 1819–1834.* New Haven: Yale University Press.

Helen E. Purkitt, Stephen F. Burgess (2001) *The Rollback of South Africa's Chemical and Biological Warfare Program.* Air University, Counterproliferation Center, Maxwell Airforce Base, Alabama.

Helen E. Purkitt, Stephen F. Burgess (2005). *South Africa's Weapons of Mass Destruction.* Indiana University Press, Bloomington.

Hitler, Adolf (1925). *Mein Kampf.* Trans. Ralph Manheim. Boston: Houghton Mifflin.

Hitler, Adolf; Trevor-Roper, Hugh (1953). *Hitler's Table-Talk, 1941–1945: Hitler's Conversations Recorded by Martin Bormann.* Oxford: Oxford University Press.

Ikeler, A. A. (1972). *Puritan Temper and Transcendental Faith: Carlyle's Literary Vision.* Columbus, OH: Ohio State University Press.

Kaplan, Robert D. (2003). *Surrender or Starve: Travels in Ethiopia, Sudan, Somalia, and Eritrea.* Vintage.

Kaplan, Robert D (2000). *The Coming Anarchy: Shattering the Dreams of the Post Cold War.* Vintage.

Kaplan, Robert D. (2001). *The Ends of the Earth: From Togo to Turkmenistan, from Iran to Cambodia--A Journey to the Frontiers of Anarchy.* Peter Smith Pub Inc.

Kater, Michael H. (2011). *The Nazi Symbiosis: Human Genetics and Politics in the Third Reich.* Bulletin of the History of Medicine 85.

Levi, Neil; Rothberg, Michael (2003). *The Holocaust: Theoretical Readings.* Rutgers University Press.

Lewis, Rupert (1982). *Walter Rodney's Intellectual and Political Thought.* Wayne State University Press.

Lusane, Clarence (2002). *Hitler's Black Victims: The Historical Experiences of European Blacks, Africans and African Americans During the Nazi Era.* Crosscurrents in African American History. Routledge: New York.

MacDougall, Hugh A. (1982). *Racial Myth in English History: Trojans, Teutons, and Anglo-Saxons.* Montreal: Harvest House & University Press of New England.

Madley, Benjamin (2005). *From Africa to Auschwitz: How German South West Africa Incubated Ideas and Methods Adopted and Developed by the Nazis in Eastern Europe.* European History Quarterly 35.

Mamdani, Mahmood (2001). *When Victims Become Killers: Colonialism, Nativism, and the Genocide in Rwanda.* Princeton University Press: Princeton.

Menand, L. (2001). *Morton, Agassiz, and the Origins of Scientific Racism in the United States*. Journal of Blacks in Higher Education.

Miller, Randall M.; John David Smith (1997). *Dictionary of Afro-American Slavery*. Westport: Praeger.

Mirza, I. A., Khan, M. A., Hakim, A. (2005). *Lassa Fever UN Peacekeepers' Nightmare in West Africa*. Pakistan Armed Forces Medical Journal (1).

Morabia, Alfredo, editor. (2004). *A History of Epidemiologic Methods and Concepts*. Basel, Birkhauser Verlag. Part I.

Morton, Samuel George (1839). *Crania Americana; or, A Comparative View of the Skulls of Various Aboriginal Nations of North and South America: To which is Prefixed An Essay on the Varieties of the Human Species*. Philadelphia: J. Dobson.

Moses, A. Dirk (2008). *Empire, Colony, Genocide: Conquest, Occupation and Subaltern Resistance in World History*. Berghahn Books,:NY

Nott, Josiah Clark (1851) *An Essay on the Natural History of Mankind, Viewed in Connection with Negro Slavery* Delivered Before the Southern Rights Association, 14 December 1850.

Nott, Josiah Clark, George R. Gliddon, Samuel George Morton, Louis Agassiz, William Usher, and Henry S. Patterson (1854) *Types of Mankind: Or, Ethnological Researches : Based Upon the Ancient Monuments, Paintings, Sculptures, and Crania of Races, and Upon Their Natural, Geographical, Philological and Biblical History*. Illustrated by Selections from the Inedited Papers of Samuel George Morton and by Additional Contributions from L. Agassiz, W. Usher, and H.S. Patterson.

Nott, Josiah Clark, George Robins Gliddon, and Louis Ferdinand Alfred Maury (1857). *Indigenous Races of the Earth; Or, New Chapters of Ethnological Inquiry; Including Monographs on Special Departments*.

Olusoga, David and Erichsen, Casper W (2010). *The Kaiser's Holocaust: Germany's Forgotten Genocide and the Colonial Roots of Nazism*. Faber and Faber.

Ratzel, Friedrich (1896) *The History of Mankind*. London: MacMillan and Co. Ltd.

Roberts, Martin (1975). *The New Barbarism – A Portrait of Europe 1900–1973*. Oxford University Press.

Rodney, Walter (1972). *How Europe Underdeveloped Africa*. London: Bogle-L'Ouverture.

Roe, Frederick William (1921). *The Social Philosophy of Carlyle and Ruskin*. New York: Harcourt, Brace & Company.

Rosenbaum, Ron (1999). *Explaining Hitler: The Search for the Origins of His Evil*. Harper Perennial.

Rothman K, Sander Greenland, Lash T, editors (2008). *Modern Epidemiology*. 3rd Edition, Lippincott Williams & Wilkins.

Scheck, Raffael (2006). H*itler's African Victims: The German Army Massacres of Black*

French Soldiers in 1940. Cambridge University Press.

Schmuhl, Hans-Walter (2003). *The Kaiser Wilhelm Institute for Anthropology, Human Heredity and Eugenics. 1927-1945.* Boston Studies in the Philosophy of Science vol. 259, Wallstein Verlag, Göttingen.

Schwalbe, G. and Eugen Fischer (eds.) (1923) *Anthropologie.* Leipzig: B.G. Teubner.

Shah, Sonia (2006). *The Body Hunters.* The New Press: New York and London.

Sharp, P. M.; Hahn, B. H. (2011). *Origins of HIV and the AIDS Pandemic.* Cold Spring Harbor Perspectives in Medicine 1.

Shelley, Baranowski (2011). *Nazi Empire: German Colonialism and Imperialism from Bismarck to Hitler.* Cambridge University Press.

Smith, Woodruff D (1980). *Friedrich Ratzel and the Origins of Lebensraum.* German Studies Review, vol.3, No.1

Steinmetz, George (2007). *The Devil's Handwriting: Precoloniality and the German Colonial State in Qingdao, Samoa, and SouthWest Africa.* University of Chicago Press.

Terry, Fiona (2002). *Condemned to Repeat: The Paradox of Humanitarian Action.* London and Ithaca: Cornell University Press.

Walraven, Klaas van (2003). *Rethinking Resistance: Revolt and Violence in African History.* Brill Academic Publishers.

Wanklyn, Harriet (1961). *Friedrich Ratzel: A Biographical Memoir and Bibliography.* London: Cambridge University Press.

Waring, Walter (1978). *Thomas Carlyle.* Boston: Twayne Publishers.

Washington, Harriet (2007). *Medical Apartheid: The Dark History of Medical Experimentation on Black Americans from Colonial Times to the Present.* Social History of Medicine: New York.

Weindling, P. (1985). *Weimar Eugenics: The Kaiser Wilhelm Institute for Anthropology, Human Heredity and Eugenics in Social Context.* Annals of Science 42 (3): 303–318

Wilkins, John S. (2008). *"Darwin". In Tucker, Aviezer. A Companion to the Philosophy of History and Historiography.* Blackwell Companions to Philosophy. Chichester: Wiley-Blackwell.

Wood, George Bacon (1853). *A Biographical Memoir of Samuel George Morton, M.D.* Philadelphia: College of Physicians of Philadelphia.

Yun, N. E.; Walker, D. H. (2012). *Pathogenesis of Lassa Fever.* Viruses 4 (12).

INDEX

Lightning Source UK Ltd.
Milton Keynes UK
UKHW041340211122
412578UK00007B/341